Litani River

This book is dedicated to the Army Commandos,
past and present.

Litani River

First published in the United Kingdom 2011.

Copyright © Ian McHarg. All rights reserved.

No part of this book may be reproduced, stored in a retrieval system or transmitted by any other means, without prior and express written permission by the author/publisher.

A catalogue record of this book is available from the British Library. ISBN 978-1-907463-38-9

For more information please visit the website:
www.litaniriver.com

CONTENTS

Acknowledgements	4
Prologue	6
The Commando Initiative – June 1940	10
Commando Training – September 1940	28
Layforce and the Glen Ships – January 1941	55
Cyprus – April 1941	68
Action at Last! – June 1941	76
Farcical Beginnings – 8 June 1941	81
Litani River: X Party – 9/10 June 1941	88
Litani River: Y Party – 9/10 June 1941	102
Litani River: Z Party – 9/10 June 1941	122
Litani River: No Quarter	147
Litani River: Recollections and Commentary	155
Epilogue	158
Notes	164
Bibliography	178

ACKNOWLEDGEMENTS

Writing this book would not have been possible but for the assistance of the surviving members of No.11 (Scottish) Commando including: Sir Tommy Macpherson, Gerald Bryan, Reg Harmer, Jimmy Storie, Jim Bogle, and Jimmy Lawson. I am also grateful for letters and correspondence from: Eric Garland, James Swanston, Jock Herd and Joe Gorman. In particular I would like to thank Sir Tommy Macpherson for allowing access to the archives in both the Imperial War Museum and the National War Museum of Scotland.

I am indebted to those I visited not only for sharing their memoirs and experiences but for their kindness and hospitality, many thanks to: Lady Macpherson, Mrs Humphries, Mrs Bryan, Mrs Hill, Reg Harmer and Jimmy Lawson. I would like to thank all the families and friends, who made telephone calls, sent emails, wrote letters, gave photographs and offered words of encouragement including: Mrs Storie, Mrs Fraser, Mrs Low, Mrs Younger, Mrs Crawford, Mrs Drummond, Mrs Highland, Mrs Noble, Josa Young, Henry More, Alan Orton, Ian Omerod-Wilkinson, Tom Herd, Mark Jennings and Mr A.J. Swanson.

I am very grateful for the assistance of Stuart Allan and the staff of the National War Museum of Scotland; Dr Roderick Bailey and staff from the Imperial War Museum; the staff of the Public Records Office; the staff of the Royal Highland Fusiliers Museum; the Commando Veterans Association; and Jessie and Spud Taylor for their assistance at the Arran Heritage Museum and for their endless enthusiasm and encouragement. I would also like to thank Dr Hamish Ross for permitting me to use transcripts from interviews for his book "Paddy

Mayne".

Finally, I would like to thank my family for their unstinting support, encouragement and patience during the writing of Litani River.

PROLOGUE

Mediterranean Sea – 9 June 1941

30 minutes to landing – "Issue the rum", was the order; tense, the men of No.11 (Scottish) Commando crouched on low narrow benches that ran the length of the Assault Landing Craft (ALC). For most this was their first taste of combat, after ten hard months of training, and many false starts, Lt Col Dick Pedder was about to lead his fledgling commandos onto the battlefield. Blinkered by the crafts high sides, the rum was a welcome tonic, but not enough to calm the nerves of even the toughest among them.

Two hours earlier they had paraded below deck aboard the converted troop carrier HMS Glengyle for a final inspection and confirmation of orders. Formed into three parties: X, Y and Z, they were to storm the beach and secure the occupied ground to allow the advancing 21st Australian Infantry Brigade to continue with its advance through Lebanon and on to Syria.

Standing in his landing craft, Dick Pedder was able to observe the other three craft that made up his Y Party. To his right and over a mile to the south, the four ALCs of Major Geoffrey Keyes's X Party were a distant blur. To the north, on Pedder's left flank, Z Party - under the command of Captain George More - were packed into three landing craft. More's party consisting of No.10 and No.4 Troops were tasked to clear the Kafr Bada bridge which crossed a rocky wadi on the main north-south highway. No.10 Troop led by 20-year-old Lt Tommy Macpherson had earlier, in complete darkness and silence, embarked onto the landing craft. Macpherson, a Cameron Highlander, had applied for Special Service while defending the Caithness coast with the 5th Camerons; a task that had not enthralled him.

On volunteering Macpherson hand picked men he thought most suitable from other companies within the Camerons, many of whom were crouched anxiously behind him aboard ALC No 2. Feeling, rather than hearing, the engines in the calm waters, the commandos knew the advantage lay with the enemy; embarkation had taken longer than expected, the full moon was setting behind them and the sun was rising into their eyes; and to make matters worse an aborted landing 24-hours earlier had alerted an enemy that had vowed to, "Fight to the last man and to the last shell."

Hands and faces blackened with burnt cork, they sat in silence, alone with their thoughts, apprehensive and excited, questioning their ability and speculating on how they would cope when at last they would come face-to-face, hand-to-hand, with the enemy. For that was the reality of the operation, they were a raiding force, without artillery or air support, no armour or heavy machine guns.

Equipped and dressed for speed and aggression, dressed in khaki shirts and shorts, rope soled boots and steel helmets camouflaged with green and brown painted sacking. Armed only with rifles, bayonets, tommy guns, pistols, grenades and knives, each man knew that as soon as the ramp was down, and they hit the open beach, urgency was vital; the longer they took to get into cover the more vulnerable they were.

10 minutes to landing – "Stand by", the order was whispered along the line in Macpherson's landing craft. Individually they played out the next few minutes in their minds each man preparing in his own way; collectively they knew exactly what was expected - Dick Pedder had ensured that. Meticulous in his preparation, ruthless with his discipline, effective with his training, he had a drilled his Commando into a competent fighting unit. However they all knew that no matter how hard the training had been they were just minutes away from the reality of battle. The thundering noise of the hull grounding on to the sandbar snapped them from their thoughts. Within seconds the ramp was lowered and a blanket of sea water greeted them - instinct told them that things weren't right, but training and discipline ensured they exited at the double. The first men off the ramp disappeared completely into the deep water. Panic ensued. To stay on the craft would have been disastrous, so they had no option but to throw themselves into the water and swim and scramble their way until their feet touched the sea bed. With the ALCs quickly reversing away, a human chain was formed and men and weapons were helped ashore. As No.10 Troop waded through the water they came under machine gun fire, returning it where possible. However the mixture of water and sand caused weapons to stop, requiring the raiders to take cover and clean their weapons. 18-year-old, Bren gunner, George Dove, the youngest commando in the Troop, was one of the first to suffer at the hands of the fortified defenders. Shot through the strap on his tin helmet, the ricocheting bullet passed through the flesh on Dove's backside. Undeterred, Dove continued firing his machine gun for the rest of the operation, but others however were less fortunate. Among the men never to get off the beach were Cpl. Robert McKay and Pte Ben Hurst both shot while in cover minutes before the whistle to advance was blown. Along the coast line the other two parties were experiencing similar situations. The first opposed landing on a hostile shore by a complete Commando Force was well under way, and Dick Pedder's No.11 Scottish Commando were about to be thrown into a baptism of fire that, for those fortunate enough to get through it, would live with them for the rest of their lives; and for those who didn't, their sacrifice would never be forgotten. This is their story.

CHAPTER 1
THE COMMANDO INITIATIVE

June – August 1940

From all over Scotland, men from the Scottish Command had answered the call for volunteers for Special Service. Over 500 men, frustrated by endless guard shifts and mundane regimental duties, converged in the Border's town of Galashiels. Craving action and adventure, they had been instructed to report to the Douglas Hotel, the temporary headquarters of No.11 (Scottish) Commando. There they were met by the imposing figure of the Commanding Officer (CO), Major Dick Pedder, a tough, uncompromising officer with over sixteen years service with the Highland Light Infantry (HLI) to his credit. Born in Southampton in 1904, Robert Richard Newsham Pedder, the son of Brigadier General Ernest Pedder, had been commissioned in July 1924, before being appointed Commanding Officer of No.11 (Scottish) Commando by the Scottish Command on 22 July 1940.[1]

Dick Pedder

Photo courtesy of
National War Museum Scotland

As the volunteers arrived in Galashiels they were temporary billeted in the nearby Netherdale Mill, a disused textile plant that the Commando had taken over from one of the many infantry regiments in the area. Conditions were primitive to say the least and few were impressed, as one volunteer would later record:

Galashiels in 1940, what a dump, disused woollen mills, every type of Regiment round the place. We finished up in Netherdale Mill...the washing facilities were awful - the latrines were pre Domesday Book - the food was atrocious - to wash our eating irons we had to use a horse trough.[2]

The comfort and privileges of the barrack life they had left behind soon became a distant memory for the Special Service volunteers. Dick Pedder had been in charge of training at the HLI Training Depot, and was considered by many to have the required credentials for the new role. This was an opinion certainly shared by his Commanding Officer, Lt Col Harry Ross-Skinner, who over thirty years later would pay tribute to Pedder's training expertise:

My officers were magnificent. This extreme cunning I attribute to a young Regular Officer of my Regiment – well, perhaps not so young – Captain Dick Pedder. He had been training officers at our depot in Maryhill, near Glasgow. I really think he was the first officer to introduce Commando style training into the British Army.[3]

To assist Pedder, Major Bruce Ramsay MC, a territorial officer from the Cameron Highlanders, was appointed Second in Command of the unit. Ramsay, a veteran of the First World War, was responsible for administrating and assembling the volunteers.

Several weeks earlier on 4 June 1940, Prime Minister Winston Churchill had written to General Lord Ismay, Head of the Military Wing of the War Cabinet Secretariat, demanding that under no circumstances would Britain resort to the defensive strategy that had failed the French, and that work was to begin immediately to organise raiding forces that would strike along the coasts of the occupied countries. Determined to take the war to the Germans, in a further minute to Ismay two days later, Churchill added that:

Enterprises must be prepared with specially trained troops of the hunter class, who can develop a reign of terror first of all on a 'butcher and bolt' policy...I look to Chiefs of Staff to propose me measures for a vigorous, enterprising and ceaseless offensive against the whole German occupied coastline, do a deep a raid inland, cutting vital communications, and then back, leaving a trail of German corpses behind them.[4]

Churchill's urgency to resolve the matter was not lost on the Chief of the Imperial General Staff, General Sir John Dill. Within days of the Prime Minister's demands, Dill had delegated the task to his Military Assistant, Lt Col Dudley Clarke, Royal Artillery, to initiate the 'butcher and bolt' policy. Clarke, who had grown up in South Africa, had a profound interest in military history and fervently recalled how the Spanish had engaged in hit-and-run raids behind enemy lines with small bands of lightly armed irregular soldiers, against the French during the Peninsular War. He recollected how the Boers had used similar tactics against the British at the end of the nineteenth century. However, it was by witnessing for himself how a handful of ill-armed Arabs, attacking by surprise and manoeuvring superbly, had tied down more than an entire Corps of regular

British Army troops in Palestine in 1936, that convinced him that this type of irregular guerrilla warfare was what was required to take the fight back to the Germans.[5] With this notion in mind Clarke declared that:

Guerrilla warfare was always in fact the answer of the ill-equipped patriot in the face of a vaster though ponderous military machine; and that seemed to me to be precisely the position in which the British Army found itself in June 1940.[6]

Clarke outlined the concept of a new breed of British soldier that would have all the attributes of the Spanish, Arabian, and Boer guerrilla fighters. For this purpose he referred to this new concept of soldiers as "The Commandos", a name borrowed from a book about the Boer Kommandos by the South African author Denys Reitz. Clarke took the one-page outline to Dill, who immediately presented the proposal to the Prime Minister. Clarke's Commando concept received the approval of Churchill, who had championed the idea of "storm troopers", having seen for himself how effective they were for the Germans in the First World War, and also from witnessing the Boer guerrillas in action during the Boer War.

Despite opposition from regular army authorities, the Chiefs of Staff instructed the five regional commands: Southern, Eastern, Western, London District and Household Division, and Scottish Command, to provide enough men for two Commandos per Command, with each Commando coming under the province of Combined Operations. By July 1940, Churchill had appointed his good friend Admiral of the Fleet, Sir Roger Keyes as Director of Combined Operations.[7] From a pool of volunteers; Commanding Officers were selected to lead the new Commando units. COs were then responsible for selecting Troop Leaders; it was these junior officers who would then select from the hundreds of volunteers Non-Commissioned Officers (NCOs) and Other Ranks (ORs) deemed suitable for Commando operations.

This selective system of reaching operational strength worked extremely well for the Commandos; with no shortage of volunteers, men of all ranks and from all cap badges were keen to escape the dull routine of wartime service. The selection process also enabled CO's and Troop Leaders to stamp their own identity on the shape and development of the unit. It would be their ability to inspire and drive their new charges that would determine the operational success of the Commando. For the new recruits of No.11 (Scottish) Commando their destiny was in good hands, Dick Pedder was an extremely detailed and single-minded officer who was determined to weld his officers and men into an effective fighting machine.

Among the first and most senior of the regular Troop Leaders selected by Dick Pedder was Geoffrey Keyes, the son of the Director of Combined Operations Sir Roger Keyes. Born in Aberdour, Fife in 1917, Keyes had attended Eton and the Royal Military Academy Sandhurst. After being commissioned into the Royal Scots Greys in February 1937 he served in Palestine and saw action at Narvik in Norway. On his return from Norway, Keyes was posted to the 3rd Cavalry Training Regiment at Redford Barracks, Edinburgh as Second in Command of a dismounted Squadron; bored and frustrated he volunteered for Special Service. On arrival at Galashiels, Keyes had brought with him a group of men, many of them instructors from the 3rd Cavalry Training Regiment. "First class chaps, who ought to be the right type," he told his father.[8] Dick Pedder understood the importance of team spirit and camaraderie, and quickly grasped Churchill's concept and vision for "specially trained troops of the hunter class". With this in mind Troops were formed around officers who had hand-picked men from their own regiments, men they knew and men they could trust. Bonds were made that would remain unbroken through war and peace and that would stand the test of time.

Geoffrey Keyes

Photo courtesy of
National War Museum Scotland

Due to the irregular and specialised role of the new Commando units, they were intentionally given a degree of flexibility in terms of administration, recruitment and training. An initial structure of a HQ and ten Troops per Commando was adopted, with each Troop led by a Captain and subdivided in turn into two Sections with each Section further divided into two sub-Sections. Sections were generally led by subalterns or senior NCOs, and sub-Sections by both senior and junior NCOs; with each Commando initially having a total war establishment of approximately 500 officers and men.

Among the youngest officers to arrive at Galashiels was 19-year-old 2nd Lt Tommy Macpherson, a Cameron Highlander who was stationed in Caithness with the 5th Battalion. The Camerons were responsible for defending the Caithness coast, a task that had not captivated the energetic Macpherson, who jumped at the opportunity for Special Service. Macpherson, who was educated at Fettes College and Trinity College Oxford, hand-picked a number of men whom he thought would be suitable for the Commandos. However the exceptional sportsman soon found that he would have to rely on the experience of a familiar face before finally getting his men. Now, Sir Tommy Macpherson, the former President of the Commando Association explained:

I volunteered and I myself picked from the other companies the other ranks that I thought suitable. I went down to Galashiels and clocked in and found that the administrative man was a Major Ramsay, who had been my Company Commander in September 1939. He was a First World War veteran with a Military Cross and one arm and so was considered the bees' knees by all concerned; he was also very convivial and liked his dram. The first thing that happened to me was that my Commanding

Officer, of the Camerons, decided that the people I picked were too good and he wasn't going to let them go and signalled that a substantially different body of men was about to be sent. I got Major Ramsay to call in higher authority and got ninety percent of the personnel I selected and they remained my Troop throughout the active period of Scottish Commando – and very good they were.[9]

Tommy Macpherson

Photo courtesy of
National War Museum Scotland

Macpherson was appointed No.10 Troop Leader, among the NCOs selected and appointed as No.1, 2, 3 and 4 Sub-Section Leaders respectively were Sgt B Wills, a professional musician before enlistment, Sgts John McCulloch and Charles Bruce - both from the Black Watch, and Sgt Edward McDonald from the 6th Battalion of the Cameron Highlanders.

Sub-sections were further broken down into designated parties each with a specific role, which generally consisted of rifle, Bren gun and bomber parties. Sgt McDonald's No.2 sub-Section consisted of the following men: rifle party - Cpl Tom Scott, who had worked as a chemist before the war; LCpl Dave Rutherford a married man from Leith and an assurance agent prior to enlistment; and Pte P. Mackintosh, a 19-year-old shepherd. All three had joined the Camerons before volunteering for Special Service. The sub-Sections Bren gun party also included two Cameron Highlanders - Ptes F. Judge, a metal polisher, and D. Kirk, an insurance agent both who had enlisted on the same day, 15 March 1940; the Bren gun party was led by Cpl A. Botherway, a married man from Nottinghamshire, who had joined the Commando from the 9th Sherwoods. Sgt McDonald's bomber party included – LCpl Neil Sproule from the 2nd Battalion the Manchester Regiment, Pte G. Patrick also from the 9th Sherwood Foresters and Pte J. Hamilton, another Cameron, who worked as a commercial traveller before joining up.

So barely six weeks after Churchill challenged his Chiefs of Staff to propose measures for a ceaseless offensive against the German-occupied coastline, volunteers from all walks of life and from a variety of regiments were gathering in their hundreds to grasp the opportunity for action and adventure. The process of self-selection was the first step for all would-be commandos; those who had voluntarily put their name forward for selection were literally taking a step into the unknown. There was no existing blue print for the Commandos', the development of the concept, and the standards for recruitment, selection and training would be determined by the Commanding Officer. However, to streamline the selection process, a criteria was set for volunteering; all potential commandos had to be trained soldiers, physically fit, able to swim and immune from sea and air sickness; their personal attributes had to include courage, physical endurance, initiative and resource, activity, marksmanship, self-reliance and an aggressive spirit towards the war.[10]

Training in Galashiels soon got under way in earnest. Reveille was set for 0630hrs followed 30 minutes later by one hour of Physical Training (PT) before returning for breakfast at 0800hrs; morning parade, followed by kit inspection, took place at 0900hrs. PT continued throughout the morning usually in the form of fast-paced 8-10 mile route marches. For those men who were capable enough to get through the coming weeks and months they would soon come to realise Dick Pedder's passion for route marching. After lunch PT would continue in the form of swimming, running and more exercising until tea time, which was followed by lectures until 1800hrs, after which, unless on company duties, their time was their own.[11] The initial intensity and frequency of the training was a shock to the system for many of the volunteers including some of the Troop Leaders. In a letter to his parents on 16 August 1940, Geoffrey Keyes, who had been appointed as No.2 Troop Leader, wrote:

We have been very busy and energetic and I am just working off my stiffness and getting fit. We march and swim and do other violent things, so one goes to bed very weary and sleeps like a log.[12]

For Dick Pedder, Galashiels was only a muster point

to raise the Commando, and was soon making plans to move the unit to a more demanding training ground on the Isle of Arran. Situated on Scotland's rugged west coast, and rising impressively from the Firth of Clyde between the Ayrshire coast and Kintyre, Arran's mountainous form dominates the open waters of the Clyde. Its jagged peaks, huge corries, and miles of rugged coastline would prove to be the ideal training ground for the Commandos. With volunteers well in excess of the 500 required for operational strength, Dick Pedder contrived a plan to separate the wheat from the chaff. No stranger to pushing men to their limits, and well-known for his 50-hours toughening exercises at the end of HLI training courses, he ordered the Commando to march the 100 miles from Galashiels to Ayr in preparation for the move to Arran. This was to be the first of many tests of physical and mental endurance that they would endure. Many of the volunteers found the march very demanding, well beyond what they had been used to, and most suffered from blisters and feet problems from the constant rubbing of their boots.

After being evacuated from Dunkirk, 20-year-old Pte Reg Harmer from the Wiltshire Regiment had been posted to Scotland. Harmer, one of many volunteers from the Wiltshires who made up No.4 Troop, recalls how some suffered:

It didn't really bother me in as much as my feet were still bad cause I had 21 days in France without taking my boots off, but being infantry I was marching, it was part of your training, but the poor Gunners and Signallers who were used to driving around in vehicles it must have been bloody hard. We used to march in a group, like a Troop there was ten Troops and he kept most of the regiments together so I had all the Wilts with me, and then there was Lincoln's, North Hants all infantry in my lot. We had one group of RA blokes who could not march or had done very little marching, when we were about three parts along the way they were knackered but their guts was there and they wanted to go all the way. We got together and said, "Come on, boys you're not going to fall out, none of us are going to leave this Troop", and we shared their kit amongst us so we got to Ayr. Yes it was tough especially when we got to the Douglas Moor, cos it was all cobbles, no road like we got nowadays, but there was a road for the truck to drive along. Anyway he (Pedder) borrowed six pipers from the Cameronians from Galashiels which was their home depot and they used to lead us in the front and every time we stopped we used to move up one place and the front Troop would go to the back. When we got to the Douglas Moor we were at the front and as we are stood there I said to some of the blokes, and they new my feelings about bagpipes, "Shit, look what we have got here right in front of us," and of course we started off and honestly we hadn't been going a mile and when you heard the pipes, you didn't march you sort of swayed and am sure it was them that bucked us up.[13]

On leaving Galashiels they followed the route to Ayr passing through Peebles, Muirkirk and Cumnock on the way. The first night they stopped at Innerleithen, grabbed some much-needed food from the Church of Scotland canteen before settling down to sleep under the stars. For four days they marched hard, washed in rivers, slept in hedgerows and ate where they could; a hard routine that typified the commando attitude. It was the challenge that most had craved and being deprived of the comforts of a barrack room never bothered them. Reg Harmer continued:

That was something that we didn't worry about with the Commandos, accommodation didn't bother us, you went and found it and if you couldn't get any you slept in the hedgerows like we did when we marched from Galashiels to Ayr, we used to sleep in the hedgerow pull your blanket around you and that was it, wake up in the morning soaking wet, put it on your pack and away you went again. It wasn't until we got to Cumnock that we had a real first-class meal and that was put on by the people of Cumnock, the miners' wives put a do on for us. I don't know who told them we were coming but it was a lovely meal and don't think it was anything special but we had been living on corned beef and biscuits it was a real feast, I shall never forget that time.[14]

As the Troops leapfrogged each other on a westerly bearing, Dick Pedder marched along side, scrutinising his officers, measuring up his men, looking for those capable and worthy of being part of his elite unit. He organised for the trucks carrying the unit's equipment to travel behind the men, sweeping up the stragglers or the injured. He permitted anybody who did not have the physical or mental endurance to complete the march to travel to Ayr in the trucks. Some who chose the easy option were quick to mock and taunt those who were still marching as they drove past. However, Dick Pedder did not suffer fools gladly and on reaching Ayr instantly issued all those who had boarded the vehicles with a Return to Unit (RTU) chit, sending them back to the dull and mundane regimental routines from which they had tried to escape; a punishment that would strike fear into the toughest among them.

Unlike most of the officers, Geoffrey Keyes did not fair so well on the march, in a letter written from Lamlash, dated 30 August 1940 he wrote:

I arrived here rather earlier than I expected as in training I strained my right achilles tendon, and got a 'filled hock'. The first day's walk was rather a shocker, as we started off from scratch with eleven miles nonstop in three hours, twenty minutes, halt for lunch, then another four miles in one hour. No joke; I finished rather lame as did most of my cavalrymen, but we got a good chit from the CO for our spirit. We slept that night under the stars in a wood after a bathe in the Tweed - pretty cold, and, next day I was incredibly stiff. The CO sent me on the next day to arrange the night's bivouac, despite my efforts to be allowed to march (as it wasn't so far and I think I could have done it). I felt pretty lousy leaving my chaps, some of whom were nearly as bad as me. That afternoon when we got into the bivouac I had prepared, I was sent on with the Second in Command right down the route.[15]

The unit arrived in Ayr on 4 September and received a good reception from the locals. Walter Marshall, a Royal Scots Greys who had followed Geoffrey Keyes into No.2 Troop, recalled that:

The people were gems - especially the girls. It was a wonderful feeling marching through Ayr behind the pipes. In the Town Hall we were given a magnificent meal. After speeches of welcome, the CO told us, the Provost and the councillors, what was expected of us. It was a very stirring speech. That night we bivouacked in Dam Park. I remember swimming nude in the River Ayr.[16]

While the rest of the unit had been on the march from Galashiels to Ayr, Tommy Macpherson and fellow officer Ian Glennie, from the Gordon Highlanders, were taking part in the first Commando Officers Course that was being held at Loch Ailort. Macpherson recalls his time on the course and his encounter with an old acquaintance from the Highlands, Simon 'Shimi' Fraser, The Lord Lovat, whose father had founded the Lovat Scouts during

Litani River

the Boer War:

> They were still very amateur because it was the very first course, Shimi Lovat was doing the field-craft, and obviously we were the only two Scottish commandos, the rest were English people, who had never done any stalking or anything like that, so Shimi pounced on me, and said, "You've got to help me on the course." So I spent two thirds of the time learning the various commando things and a third as assistant to Shimi up the hill.
>
> We had two extraordinary ex-Shanghi policemen, Fairburn and Sykes. I certainly will never forget them, partly because they were amazing and partly because of the first time I met Sykes - they were quite small, very broad chaps, he (Sykes) put out a hand in welcome and the next thing I new I was flat on my back over his shoulder, and he said, "That's your first lesson, you've got to be ready for anything all the time."
>
> Then we had a First World War, Scots Guard Officer, called Mackworth Pread, who was a weapon's specialised, and he was the finest bolt action rifle shot I've ever seen. He could get twenty shots in the bull at 300 yards in a minute, he really was extraordinary. We had a very good explosive chap and a gentleman on release from Peterhead Jail who was an expert safe man, and a very nice chap he was too.[17]

CHAPTER 2
COMMANDO TRAINING – ISLE OF ARRAN

September 1940

On 6 September the Commando disembarked at Lamlash, where they were marched from the pier and divided into groups for billeting in the homes of the residents of the small town. Major Ramsay had put Geoffrey Keyes in charge of the billeting arrangements; officers were given a daily allowance of 13/4d while the other ranks were allowed 6/8d. Several weeks earlier the ladies of Lamlash have been invited to attend a special meeting in the public hall where the speaker was Dick Pedder. He explained to them that the west coast of Scotland had been chosen as the training ground for special service troops; and that he had come to ask for their cooperation in billeting his men by offering to take as many into their houses as they could accommodate, adding that if, he didn't get the cooperation he was looking for, the houses would be requisitioned anyway!

The officers meanwhile rented the White House from the Duchess of Montrose to use as an Officer's Mess. Geoffrey Keyes had quickly settled into his new surroundings and was soon enjoying his time on Arran. In a letter to his father he wrote:

> I and my two officers live in a charming little cottage not far from the White House, where we are very comfortable. The troops are in the surrounding houses so we are very handy. The chaps are being looked after very well by all the old bodies here who feed them very well, and it is a superb place. They are

enjoying themselves a lot.[1]

Fellow officer 2nd Lt Blair 'Paddy' Mayne, was also settling in on the island; billeted at Landour, in a letter he wrote to his mother, he described their living quarters:

> I like this place - we are very comfortable here and the mess is fine. I don't live in the mess as I think I told you. Five of us are in a small parlour house, only for sleeping of course. I prefer it. We keep a fire going, have a gramophone, and there is a pot of tea made in the evening. I think this is the sort of place I'll live in. No women about it, and clothes lying about all over the place, dirty teacups on the floor, wet boots in the oven, a rugby jersey over one armchair and your feet on the fender, a perfect existence. We have lots of labour saving devices also, e.g. the coal is in very large lumps. To split it we just fire a revolver shot into it, it cracks it wonderful.[2]

Paddy Mayne, a huge man from Newtonards in Northern Ireland, was appointed No.7 Troop Leader by Dick Pedder. Educated at Queen's University in Belfast. Mayne was a prominent rugby player as well as the Irish Universities heavyweight boxing champion, before qualifying as a solicitor. An outstanding athlete and natural leader it was on the rugby field where he excelled; capped six times for Ireland and thought by many to be the outstanding player on the victorious British Lions tour of South Africa in 1938. The following year Mayne joined the local 5th Light Anti-Artillery Territorial Regiment, before transferring to the Royal Ulster Rifles (RUR) in April 1940. It was during his time with the RUR that Mayne became close friends with 2nd Lt Eion McGonigal, who like Mayne was a keen rugby player and had also studied law at Queens University; bored and frustrated the two men volunteered for a detachment with the Cameronians (Scottish Rifles) and it was there that they read the circular requesting volunteers for Special Service, and they both duly applied for service with the Scottish Commando.

Eion McGonigal

Photo courtesy of
National War Museum Scotland

Blair Mayne

Photo courtesy of
National War Museum Scotland

As the officers and men were finding their feet in Lamlash, Tommy Macpherson had completed the Commando Course at Loch Ailort and was heading to Arran to rejoin the unit. However, as Macpherson recalls the journey to Arran was not without incident:

> I went down in a serious of trains and changed at Glasgow. The trains were running very late and the last boat had gone when I got to Gourock. It was very late and a dark night and I bumped into a policeman and said, "Where shall I go?" and he said, "Come with me," and I had an extremely comfortable night in the cells, complete with bed sheet, blankets and first-class bacon and egg breakfast, courtesy of the police.[3]

Like Macpherson, the commandos in Lamlash were also enjoying the delights of the local hospitality; Jimmy Lappin, a Cameron Highlander, who was part of Macpherson's No.10 Troop, recalled many years later:

> In the first billet I was assigned to there was only one double bed for two of us and my billet was changed to Cul-a-Valla with Mary McKechnie. Some of the lads just had a plain tea the first night and had arranged to move out but next day Mary explained that she had to wait for our ration cards. The food was great. She was a great cook and really looked after us; drying our kit and giving us hot baths.[4]

The men billeted in the town or nearby farms, were looked after by local families and mothered by welcoming landladies. Permanently wet uniforms were dried and hungry young men were fed and watered. With up to four men in a billet space was tight and strict routines had to be adhered to. Cold water was used mainly for ablutions and in some cases, for bathing. They used part of farm building, boiling up water in old set boilers and taking baths in turn, with the last man left to swill the place out. Reg Harmer, who stayed with the McCall family, recalls how they fitted in:

I stayed with Ma McCall, and her daughter Jessie, who was 15. Ma had that much faith in me that when there was a dance on, she would tell Jessie, who was dancing mad that, "Yes you can go to the dancing but only if Reg comes and picks you up." [5]

Jessie McCall, now Jessie Taylor, recalls that on one such occasion when she was all dressed up and ready to go out dancing, Reg picked her up and put her over the sink and turned the tap on over her head. Such was the relationship between the commandos and the people of Lamlash that they were soon treated like sons and brothers and truly embraced by the island communities.[6] For some ladies however looking after the commandos was a bit more than they were used to. Mary Crawford, a young married woman, explained:

From looking after and cooking for one man I found myself looking and cooking for another six. I received twenty-five shillings per week per head plus ration books. For this they had four meals a day and if they were out training in the hills they got iron rations with them. I had three boys from Newfoundland, one from Yorkshire, one from Edinburgh and a Fifer. When the two Scots boys got into an argument, their accents grew broader and broader and so I acquired another job – as an interpreter. One day Captain Keyes called to see me and said that he hoped that each boy would have a bath at least once per week. The boys paid me sixpence each time they had a bath, as you can imagine to keep the hot water flowing for three or four baths per evening meant that the coal just disappeared up the chimney like magic. In the row of ten houses only two had paths, No.10 and mine at No.5, so it was not only the boys who were billeted with me who required baths.[7]

The regimental routine for the officers and men of the Commando was quite different to that from the regiments which they had left behind. With the men in billets there were no requirements for a cook house or cooks, as breakfast and evening meals were provided by the families that they were accommodated with. There was no regimental headquarters so paperwork and administration was kept to a minimum; Troop Leaders and officers had practically no administration duties to carry out at all as virtually all were dealt with by Major Ramsay or the Adjutant, Captain George More, Royal Engineers.

More, the son of a naval officer and grandson of a Scottish naval surgeon, had been Mentioned in Dispatches in France in 1940 for his part in the evacuation of Allied troops from the beaches around Dunkirk. Utilising the full range of skills required by sapper officers he demolished bridges in the path of the advancing Germans; constructed an improvised pier of lorries, on a beach without a jetty; and later evacuated his severely wounded Commanding Officer and ten of his company on a folding boat. On return to Britain, More volunteered for Special Service and was soon posted to the Scottish Commando.

George More

Photo courtesy of
Henry More

With the unit settled in on the island, training soon got under way in earnest, and Dick Pedder was determined to produce an elite unit and was very clear on Churchill's vision for the Commandos. He was extraordinarily detailed in his approach to commando training and set about the task in an almost tyrannical manner. He was a tough and uncompromising leader who had the respect of both his officers and men, but as with all men of that nature he was not always liked. Not that that would have bothered Pedder - his singled-minded approach to training the unit was his only priority. Elizabeth Keyes recalls that her brother Geoffrey described Pedder as a man with:

Decided views of his own, who would stand no nonsense from red-tape wallahs, or anyone else for that matter; he knew exactly what he wanted, and ruthlessly culled and returned to their units those he did not want.[8]

Dick Pedder had overall responsibility for the training, but would leave the decisions regarding certain situations and tasks in the hands of his Troop Leaders and officers; he would not interfere with their judgements but would not be afraid to jump on them if he thought it was warranted.

We had to pass muster with Pedder, over the period of Commando training in Arran, we got to know him very well – all of us. Nobody liked him; he was an unlikeable man; he was a loner; he was extremely authoritarian with a quick temper.[9] He was a dictator, there was no question of that and I think that it is arguable that he tended to select rather compliant people to be Company Commanders and so on; he didn't want any talking back at all, recalled Tommy Macpherson.[10]

Whether he was liked or not, was of no relevance to Dick Pedder, he had a job to do and not much time to do it; shaping the unit into an elite fighting force was his remit and it was a task that he relished. Keen to instil the need for self-discipline and individual responsibility on his men, he started with first parades: each morning they were left to their own devices to get them selves on parade on time. This unconventional start to the daily routine was not the only changes from the norm that the commandos were to experience.

Training varied from individual, to small groups and then into large groups. Physical fitness and realistic scenarios were heavily incorporated into every task at every opportunity, and all the time Dick Pedder would be with them driving them harder than they had been driven before. Reg Harmer, who by then had been promoted to Corporal, recalls a training exercise where he failed to apply enough realism into his actions, which resulted in a tongue lashing from his Commanding Officer:

He gave me several bollockings for different things, like one time we went over the hills doing this bloody night job, you see we were coming down the road doing an exercise on the way back, it was bitterly cold and wet, 1940 was a wet season up there, when I first went there I thought Christ what have we got here because it never stopped raining. I had the Boys anti tank rifle and put myself on to a position on the road, well I was laying on the top, there was a big gully to my side and there was four foot of water in it, so I'm lying on the top of the road and along comes Pedder and he shouts, "Corporal Harmer what do you think you are doing?" "Covering this road, Sir," I reply.

"A very good idea but there's a sniper down there, and if you don't watch it he is going to have you, why don't you get in that hole?"

"Because it's full of water, Sir"
"That makes no difference, your life's at stake, get in the hole."
And I had to get in the hole, right up to my chest it was; but he was fair, several times he had a go at me, but he did with everybody, well that was his job. He would take it out on his officers if it went wrong and he thought they could have put it right, and that's why he wasn't liked by some of them, but others they liked him. In my opinion he was a fair man, I mean I was in the army before the war, you see COs then bought there commission they didn't really get it, but Pedder was in charge of the HLI training depot before he joined us and of course he was a real soldier he had done a lot of soldiering and he was a bloke who knew his drill, yes we had other officers who weren't quite up to his standard, but in my opinion he was good. He was very experienced and you couldn't have had a better regiment for experience than the HLI - Hell's Last Issue![11]

Despite the dreadful weather they were experiencing, training continued regardless and the north highlands of Arran at that time of the year could be a wild and unforgiving place; nevertheless day after day and night after night they marched and manoeuvred over mountains and through glens; they forded rivers in full spate; repeated beach landings night after night; and took frequent trips off the end of the pier in full kit, ensuring that most days they would return to their billets soaking wet, much to the displeasure of the landladies who were left with the task of drying their kit.

In a letter to his mother headed "Sunday Night, Machrie Bay" Paddy Mayne recalled one such experience of what the Arran weather was like during an endurance march in late 1940:

We left Lamlash about two o'clock and walked over here, about seventeen miles. For the first four miles there were odd showers. They didn't hinder us much since we quickly dried, but after it wasn't so good as the final shower lasted for the last thirteen miles, and there was a regular gale blowing off the sea into our faces. I waded through a river the other night and I don't think it was any wetter! This book (the letter was written on blotched sheets torn from a squared notebook) was in my pocket and is still wet. We got in here about seven o'clock and then started to find somewhere to sleep. We were carrying nothing except some food; we would not demean ourselves by carrying blankets. It is a smallish hamlet, eight or nine houses and I started going to them to find somewhere for my twenty-five men to dry their clothes. They were all decent, one old lady reminded me of you. I knocked at the door and the girl who opened it seemed scared. I think at first she thought I was a Jerry parachutist, though Father Christmas would have been more like the thing, what with all the equipment I had on. At any rate, I told her who we were, that we intended sleeping out and wondered if she could get some clothes dried. She rose to her feet. "You'll not stop outside as long as I've a bed in my house," she declared, and then went into a huddle with her two daughters and her clatter of children and then announced that she could take six. To cut a long story short, I am sitting in borrowed pyjamas and an overcoat made for a much smaller man than myself, so much so that when one of my lads saw me he said, "Let Burton dress you!" [12]

Physical Training consisted mainly of cross country runs and marches. They were expected to maintain the same speed up hill as on the flat or downhill, from Lamlash they would head to Whiting Bay then up the Ross Road before striking off to the left and up the great hill side, through moor and bog until they reached the loch on the top, and back again. More times than they could remember Pedder would send them to the top of Goat Fell, the islands highest peak. Often wet and exhausted they would return to the billets and the welcoming landladies only to be turned around and sent to the summit again, returning in the middle of the night and up again for reveille to start it all again. The island was an ideal place for a Commando to train, with flat country in the south, rolling country in the middle and steep mountainous country in the north. The sea shores and shingle beaches were perfect for all forms of amphibious training whether it was diving in full kit off the pier or swimming to Holy Isle and back; the options were plenty and the training was unyielding.

This ideal location was perfect for Pedder's unorthodox approach to training the Commando; the unit was among the first to train with live ammunition, much of which was often fired over their heads during exercises and drills. They were also often seen and heard carrying out live mortar practice on the moor between Sannox and Corrie. Unlike in their stricter regimental systems the commandos had easier access to ammunition and explosives, much of which was often stowed away under their beds in the billets, much to the annoyance of many of the landladies. Reg Harmer recalls:

> Ma McCall was a lovely woman, her only rule was no ammunition in the house, and, "I'm not having any ammunition in there, Reg," she would say. We were in the back house which was only a wooden shack, if she had only looked under the beds! I had cases and cases of .303 and 50 anti tank and a couple of boxes of hand grenades. We always used to take a few bandoliers when we went out with us; we never had any blanks only live ammo all the time.[13]

Rifles and other weapons were also the personal responsibility of the men, who would often participate in extra practise in their own time. Harmer continues:

We did most of our training up on the back hills, so we used to get up there and shoot and at the weathervane which stood on the top of the church and as it twirled in the wind we would shout, "Moving target," and fire at it, we had 2 or 3 hits on it. For years after the war we use to return to Lamlash and weathervane used to sit on the window sill inside the church.[14]

In a letter on 4 November 1940, Geoffrey Keyes could not hide his enthusiasm and excitement about how the training was going:

I am in a beastly fit and hearty state, and we sail over the local hills at great speed. We (that is the troop leaders) fire live rounds at our soldiery now to impress them of the horrors of war, and make them utilise the best cover. Most instructive and effective and brightens up training no end. We are just commencing our Aquatic Sports – yesterday I bathed my whole troop in the sea with their naval water wings on.[15]

Geoffrey Keyes was not alone in introducing his troop to the ice cold waters of the Firth of Clyde. Paddy Mayne was equally keen to adopt the seaborne role and was seen on many occasions marching No. 7 Troop off the Lamlash pier, with the rugby internationalist marching straight in behind them. This was the sight that met Piper Jimmy Lawson of the Gordon Highlanders, on his arrival at Lamlash in the autumn.

I was standing at the window of the digs and was watching a Troop marching a long the road. They turned down the old pier blowing up their Mae Wests then jumped off the pier and swam ashore. I was convinced I was in a madhouse.[16]

Jimmy Lawson

Photo courtesy of
Jimmy Lawson

Physical fitness and weapon handling was fundamental training for all infantry soldiers. However, the Commandos remit was more than that and specialised training was introduced to prepare them for the irregular type of warfare that they were expecting to undertake. Pedder was intent on giving his unit the best training possible, so when it was brought to his attention that a rock climbing specialist from No.9 Commando, stationed along the coast in Whiting Bay, was giving a demonstration of how to scale cliffs and mount an assault under the cover of darkness, he made sure he was there to observe.

Suitably impressed by the climbing and leadership skills of Lt Gerald Bryan, Royal Engineers, and his team, Pedder arranged for Bryan to be seconded to his unit in order to train a number of the men in rock climbing techniques. However, a secondment to the Commando would require more than climbing ability alone, and before Bryan was fully accepted he was required to run and march over 35 miles of Arran's coast and mountain roads. By December 1940 Gerald Bryan had been invited to join No.11 (Scottish) Commando on a permanent basis.[17]

Gerald Bryan

Photo courtesy of
National War Museum Scotland

Pedder was keen to instil the need for self-reliance on his men and insisted that they carry certain objects in certain pockets of their battledress. Items such as toilet paper, first-aid bandages, lengths of string and cheese wire had to be carried at all times and it was not unusual for him to stop a man and ask him to produce any one of the items. In another example of the level of detail that Pedder went to, he instructed each man to carry a flask of whisky and morphia tablets as part of their personal equipment, a well as a short length of rope with a bight at one end and a toggle at the other. These short lengths of ropes could be joined together for climbing cliffs or for making rope bridges, or as safety-lines for crossing fast flowing rivers. Dick Pedder was prepared to leave no stone unturned to ensure that his unit was as prepared and professional as it could be.

As the training increased in intensity and duration Pedder could see the Commando starting to shape into the elite unit that he had envisaged, but his standards were of the highest order and there was to be no let up for his men. However, he was as equally demanding on himself as he was on them; a man who believed in leading by example, he would never ask them to do anything that he couldn't do himself.

Like Pedder, The Director of Combined Operations, Sir Roger Keyes, was also determined to develop the Commandos into well drilled, professional fighting units, and was committed to using his vast naval experience in order to improve their boat handling and seamanship. He appointed his old friend Admiral Sir Walter Cowan K.C.B., C.B., D.S.O. to assist him with the task, despite being nearly seventy-years-old the Admiral was still fit and hardy, and night after night the two friends could be seen standing on the beach in all weathers waiting for the improvised landing craft to hit the shores around Lamlash Bay and Clauchlands Point, where Keyes would often be heard to say, "Far too much noise – you must do it again"; and do it again they did until he was satisfied with their performance and they had learned to keep "as quiet as mice".[18] Sir Walter was highly impressed by what he saw, and later wrote:

Coming back after a night landing and a mountain to climb at speed they would, at dawn, making for the beaches and breakfast, come in perhaps seven miles with full equipment machine guns and all, averaging five and a half miles an hour without effort, not a man falling out... ...the training of the two Scottish Commandos 9 and 11 in Arran during the autumn and winter of 1940 was the most vigorous and ruthless I have ever seen...the pick of the Scottish regiments, and they laughed at hardship - wet through at least five days out of seven and often up to or over the waist...they practiced landing in merchant ship life boats, heavy and unhandy to a degree. Most of the men had next to no knowledge of boat work, and started learning to pull in these unwieldy craft with heavy oars - it was a wonder it didn't break their hearts. Then someone has a brainwave. They took the paddles from Carley floats and went like the wind with them. The landings were mostly on shelving beaches and because of the tides the boats had to be hauled well up, which meant men being up to their waists in water. To do it in the small landing craft of course was child's play but they were not often allowed them because of the wear and tear and shortage of these craft. Sometimes the weather became very bad before they were ready to re-embark, and one evening it so happened that we might easily have drowned two boatloads in the primitive life boats - unable to make headway and drifting broadside on to the boom at the harbour entrance. I have never forgotten it. In the end, and in the nick of time, a harbour steam launch fetched out and clawed them off but only just.[19]

Reg Harmer remembers that was not the only close encounter during the amphibious training:

We didn't have landing craft we had cast-iron ship's lifeboats with these bloody great oars about sixteen feet long that we used to stick them in the water to row. We had three boats and they were lashed together, the "lazy ones" we used to call them used to get in the middle boat and the ones on the outside had to do all the work not only did you have to row it you had to get it a shore and all, we used to stick these oars in the water and as you was pulling it out you went up like that, you literally came out of the seat and went up in the air. When we neared the beach the outside boats had to bail out grab hold of the boats and run like hell and get them up onto the beach. Well one night we did a landing on the Holy Isle, during the day a hell of a storm broke out; we used to leave two boys with the boat that was supposed to be the guard, as soon as you were on enemy territory you would leave two blokes to guard the boats, and that's what we did, even though it was an exercise. So we went up and over Holy Isle and down the other side and when we came back the two boys were there but the boats were further inland, the sea had came in and lifted the boats up into the next set of rocks, retired Admiral Cowan, who was the liaison between the Army and the Navy, was with us, and he said, "Don't worry boys, come on," so we got on this bloody great rock, "stand by the boats all of you, I will count 1,2,3 and as I say 3 you lift them all off and we will be away." Well this went on for ages, and of course as we lifted up the waves came in, and we went flying and the boats went further up on to the rocks! In the end they had to send a tug over and shoot a line ashore and we had to go over the rope back to the boat. In the mean time all our landladies, now remember that we were not related to these women or there families, were all down on the pier head, lashing Pedder to hell, "Do something then those poor boys will get pneumonia." It was November mind and it was bloody cold in the water, and they are having a right old ding dong back there with Pedder, eventually the Navy had to come and get them off, and when we got back Pedder ordered all of us to have a rum issue.[20]

Despite the different assortment of regiments and nationalities that had mustered in Galashiels in the summer it was clear that they had gelled together into a proud unit without any animosity, and indeed the non-Scots amongst them soon turned out to be very proud of their new found Scottishness. It was during the process of fostering the esprit de corps attitude that Pedder introduced a uniformal headdress for the unit. He chose the Balmoral with a distinctive black hackle supported by the cap badge of the soldier's parent unit. In a letter to his father Geoffrey Keyes was keen to express his pride in his new unit:

The whole outfit is getting together well, and we all look more or less alike now, as we have got standardized equipment. The officers all have; and the men will have bonnets with large black hackles in the side. These are very smart but a bit embarrassing to the Sassenach officers...They are a grand lot, and we couldn't have a better lot of chaps...I hope, Pop, you are impressed with our fellow Commandos.[21]

This was a sentiment shared by Tommy Macpherson who would later comment that: 'I think we formed a remarkable spirit in the Commando all together'. [22]

By the autumn of 1940, the threat of an invasion by the Germans was reaching fever pitch. As part of the defence of Britain the unit left their training base on Arran and were deployed to Montrose, where some found accommodation in a local malt store, before a final move to Brechin where accommodation was found in the Mechanics Institute or with local families. Training continued; punishing runs and hours at Arbroath rifle range filled the time in between defensive duties. On one occasion, after a day off duty and a good night at the local pub, Dick Pedder laid on a surprise night exercise for his unexpectant men. A former No.2 Troop veteran recalls the night:

Dragged out of the billet between midnight and 01.00hrs after having been off duty that day, and a good night at the local. Our troop had to fall in, in battle order and moved off at the double – what a wonderful way to move a load of beer. We left the main road and into a plantation having to stay covered – had to move into some spot lord knows where – in and out of drainage dykes. Day light came and we had to cross the River South Esk in full spate and the bank was rather steep. In the river was the Colonel up to his chest in water. We had a very small chap in our Troop – 4 feet and 11 and a half inches – two of us had to hold him above the water, when we had crossed the Colonel grabbed our wee fella and said, "You three are dead." We returned to life faster than the speed of light and wet through or not I bet we beat any time trial there was for finding our way back to the billet. [23]

Reg Harmer also recalls the events of another night exercise during their time in Brechin:

One night when we were there all the talk was that the Germans were coming, possibly over from Norway; at 2 o'clock one night Piper Lawson was running around the town in a taxi blowing assembly on his bugle, so we all had to get bloody dressed in call out clobber, rifles the lot and rush down the road to the assemble point. We then marched towards Montrose and on the way there was this dilapidated old building, so we laid a few charges on it and blew it up, course what we didn't know was that while we were doing that the Germans had followed the RAF in to Montrose airport, and as they landed the Germans bombed the airfield which coincided with us blowing up the building! Of course all the people in Brechin thought that the Germans had invaded and it caused a right panic.[24]

As the threat of invasion passed the unit soon returned to Arran and training continued unabated. By this time the elderly Major Bruce had left the unit and the newly promoted Captain Geoffrey Keyes took over as Second in Command of the Commando. During November, in an attempt to reduce the mass of organisations responsible for special operations, the Commando units were reorganized into Special Service Battalions as part of the Special Service Brigade under the command of the highly decorated Brigadier Charles Hayden, Irish Guards. No.9 Commando and No.11 (Scottish) Commando were merged with men from the No.6 and No.7 Independent Companies and reconstituted as 2 Special Service Battalion.[25] However, the new battalions did not prove to be a success and Hayden strongly recommended a return to the small Commando units. Part of the unpopularity of the Special Service Battalions was the abbreviated 'SS' title and its inevitable association with the German units of the same initials.

With the reinstatement of the Commando designation, Dick Pedder was satisfied that the unit was taking shape and that they were a capable and competent fighting force, but he also understood that his men were at their peak physically and were keen to see some action. Sir Roger Keyes was busy trying to find a suitable operation that would require the Commando's expertise; towards the end of October he proposed to the Chiefs of Staff that the Commandos should be used to capture the Italian island of Pantelleria, located in the Mediterranean Sea south west of Sicily. Keyes was convinced that capturing the heavily fortified island was the key to the Central Mediterranean,[26] and by November the plans for Operation Workshop had been approved in principle by the Chiefs of Staff. Having endured months of physical and mental hardship, the frustration of the lack of action was starting to tell on the unit. In a letter dated the 19 November 1940, Geoffrey Keyes wrote to his father:

The men are longing for a show...One troop has gone away for a boating holiday, and the rest are pretty jealous and excited. If we have to wait till January, we will be a flop, for an absolute certainty. Men are asking to go back to their units so that they can go to the Middle East to fight. It is all disappointing, so please fix us up Pop. This leave business has cheered them up for the moment, but they should be exercised on their return, and they'd beat anyone living. [27]

However, with the Commando embarked and ready to sail on the 14th of December and much to everyone's frustration Operation Workshop was postponed. It was believed that the island could not be held without strong air support, which at that time was not available. Opposition for the operation from Admiral Andrew Cunnigham, Royal Navy, Commander-in-Chief of the Mediterranean Fleet, also meant that much needed destroyers would not be available for the action.

CHAPTER 3
LAYFORCE AND THE GLEN SHIPS

January 1941

Much to the frustration of all involved the initial "butcher and bolt" concept of the Commandos rampaging around European coastlines had failed to materialise. However the opportunity to utilise their training and commitment was soon to arise in the Middle East. Roger Keyes was still pushing for the capture of Pantelleria and after months of planning it seemed that 'Workshop', the on-off operation, would finally get the go ahead. On 29 January 1941 the commandos embarked in their designated ships, but once again to their utter disbelief, no sooner had they embarked than the operation was cancelled.

However, the Middle East was where the Commandos were destined for and two days later on 31 January 1941 No.11 (Scottish) Commando, No.7 Commando and No.8 Commando set sail from the Isle of Arran on board the three 'Glen' ships; HMS Glenearn, HMS Glenroy and HMS Glengyle. Five Troops from No.11 (Scottish) Commando were on board the Glenroy with Dick Pedder, and were accompanied by No.8 Commando. The remaining five Troops were aboard the Glengyle under the command of Geoffrey Keyes and accompanied by No.7 Commando. On board the Glenearn were officers and regular soldiers bound for the Middle East, as well as a Troop from Lt Col John Durnford-Slaters No.3 Commando.

The three Commando units aboard the Glengyle and the Glenroy were combined together into what was known as Force "Z", under the command of Lt Col R.E. Laycock, Royal Horse Guards, who prior to his appointment had been the Commanding Officer of No.8 Commando. For security reasons the three Commando units Nos. 7, 8 and 11 were re-named A, B and C Battalions, "Layforce" respectively.

Commandeered by Roger Keyes, the Glen ships had been specially converted to accommodate the amphibious role of the Commandos. HMS Glengyle, built by the Caledon Shipbuilding and Engineering Company in Dundee for the Glen Line, was taken over by the Admiralty in November 1939 and converted into Fleet Supply Ship before again being converted into a Landing Craft Carrier by the renowned shipbuilders John Brown and Co. Ltd. Formally known as a Landing Ship Infantry Large (LSI(L)), the converted Glengyle was commissioned into service on 10 September 1940, capable of carrying 700 military personnel, 12 Assault Landing Craft (ALC) and 2 Motor Landing Craft (MLC). The Glengyle's sister ships, HMS Glenroy and HMS Glenearn, also went through similar conversions before they too were commissioned into service. As the ships left Arran they formed part of a larger convoy which passed the north of Ireland, going west to the mid Atlantic in a gale before heading due south at a top speed of about 23 knots.[1] Conditions on board the ships took a bit of getting used to. The men slept in hammocks in what was previously the hold, and many were suffering from sea sickness and illness. By the time the convoy reached the level of Gibraltar the weather broke and the calmer waters allowed the commandos to resume their physical and military training. The days were passed carrying out weapons training, which included shooting at bottles thrown overboard, compass work and signalling courses; on the Glengyle Geoffrey Keyes set aside time to learn Italian and German, and the ever energetic Tommy Macpherson took responsibility for physical training. Evenings were passed with lectures and briefings; they entertained themselves with card schools, tombolas and concerts; sporting competitions were arranged and boxing competitions were watched by the CO.

The convoy's first scheduled stop was Freetown, Sierra Leone on 10 February 1941. Aboard the Glenroy land was sighted at approximately 1015 hrs and by 1030 hrs, in terrific heat, the commandos were lined up for parade on the ships Poop and Well decks.[2] With the men dismissed and the ship at anchor, fresh water and vegetables were re-supplied, but no shore leave had been granted so the men occupied themselves by sunbathing and fishing, or by throwing coins into the water for the local boys in canoes to dive for. During the afternoon Dick Pedder and George More boarded the Glengyle and met with Geoffrey Keyes before returning to the Glenroy by mid afternoon reporting that all was well. With blackout not till 2200hrs many slept on the decks with the Freetown lights shining in the background. From Freetown the convoy continued south crossing the equator on 13 February carrying out traditional Crossing the Line ceremonies as they went. On 19 February, eight days after leaving Freetown, the ships reach Cape Town by 0700hrs; sailing into the bay they were met by the unforgettable sight of Table Mountain. By 1030hrs the ships were docked and within two hours the commandos were lined up on the quay in full kit ready for a 12 mile speed march through the centre of Cape Town and up and over the pass between Table Mountain and the Lion Head before retuning back to the ships.

Received with incredible enthusiasm, the force also took part in a march through the town wearing for the first time First World War Indian Army topees with the Black Hackle inserted in it, taking the salute from the town Mayor. With the formalities over and the parade fell out, the town's people descended on the commandos, with each taking two or three of the men away for hospitality.³ Reg Harmer recalls his time on Cape Town:

When we got to Cape Town we had three days there, and had a wonderful time, my old mate Reggie Walters and me, we came off the boat and this bloke was standing there: "Good morning, boys, would you like a tour around?" he asked. "Yes please, sir," we replied. A Dutchman he was, a Boer. "Come on get in the car, here you are, do you smoke?" He gave us a box of fifty fags straight away, and then took us all around, stopped for lunch, glorious lunch we had, then we went off and saw some of the wild animals, then back for dinner, glorious dinner in his house, waited on and everything else...and then he took us back to the ship. We went with him for the next two days; we had a wonderful time in Cape Town.⁴

On 21 February they left the Cape and set sail once again, enduring a stormy passage towards the Red Sea. A report of a sighting of the German pocket-battleship Admiral Scheer, caused the escorting cruiser HMS Dorsetshire to leave the convoy, which headed for the safety of Durban. But the Dorsetshire soon returned and the convoy continued without stopping at Durban, with the cruiser being replaced by the cruiser HMS Glasgow just before they crossed the equator for the second time on 28 February. On 4 March the convoy sailed through the Gulf of Aden, sighting land on the starboard side as they proceeded up the Red Sea. With the welcome sight of land on both quarters they put into Port Suez at 1630hrs on 7 March and were anchored within the hour.⁵ The following day No.9 Troop were able to visit HMS Glasgow, and despite temporary repairs, were able to see for themselves the damage caused to the cruiser when it had previously been hit by two aerial torpedoes when it had been attacked by Italian aircraft while anchored in Suda Bay in Crete a few months earlier. Early on the morning of 10 March the Glen Ships entered the Suez Canal and sailed for Geneifa on the Great Bitter Lake as preliminary orders for the disembarkation of stores and personnel was issued.[6] Tommy Macpherson recalls that the journey up the canal was not without incident:

> We were to go in to Suez but we were halted on the Egyptian side, we were held around there because there was an air raid on the canal, which turned out to be nothing, but we were kept there and I remember that because, as we were disembark happy, we could clean out the galley and so forth, and we got a meat hook with a joint of beef on the end of that and caught us a shark, hauling this out and getting it on deck, we didn't know what to do with it so we shot it! [7]

At 0900hrs the following day the commandos commenced disembarking from their ships and were ready to start the march to their new tented camp shortly after 1100hrs. Within two days of entering the camp the Commando or 'C' Battalion, Layforce as it was then called, received a visit from General Wavell, General Officer Commanding the Middle East, and General Sir John Dill, Chief of the Imperial General Staff, who at been instrumental at the inception of the Commando initiative.

Training continued while they were camped at Genefia, and exercises were carried out with an invasion of an island in mind. Italian POW's were tasked to dig a replica coastline in the desert sand and mock raids were carried out on the improvised coast. The unit soon got to experience the harsh realities of desert life, as they exercised on the improvised coastline they were hit by a fierce sand storm, followed by a second that eliminated the make shift coastline, with visibility so poor that at times they had to find their way back to camp using a compass. All the time, and in spite of the rumours of a raids on the Greek island of Rhodes and the Dodecanese, they were still no closer to seeing any action as they were when they departed the shores of Arran six weeks earlier. As training and exercising continued the unit also carried out general fatigue duties while in the tented camp, one of which was unloading a ship that had arrived from Britain containing much needed sandbags, which, to their disbelief were full with sand.[8] With no operation imminent the commandos were granted leave, many including Geoffrey Keyes, who had just been promoted to Acting Major, headed for Cairo, taking time to visit the pyramids, ride camels, and leave their mark on the bars and clubs in the Egyptian capital.

After the success of Operation Compass fortunes were soon to take a turn for the worse for the Allies in North Africa. Over a ten week period from 9 December 1940 to 7 February 1941 British Forces under General O'Connor had recapture Sidi Barrani and Sollum in Egypt, before driving Marshal Rodolfo Graziani's Italian Tenth Army all the way to Beda Fomm in western Cyrenaica capturing Bardia, Tobruk and 130,000 prisoners on the way. However the introduction of General Erwin Rommel and his Afrika Korps and the untimely redeployment of British troops to Greece soon changed the situation for the worse. Sent to North Africa to rescue the Italians, Rommel grabbed his chance when British defences were at their weakest, and despite orders to the contrary attacked Bengahzi on 31 March 1941. With all his men back from leave, and in light of the developments in the western desert, Pedder was concerned about the security situation in the region, so much so that he issued a Special Order to the unit:

THE SCOTTISH 'C' BATTALION – LAYFORCE
SPECIAL ORDER

With the approach of specialised training for our specific operation, a certain amount of speculation, criticism and discussion by all ranks is inevitable. In fact constructive criticism and reasonable discussion are to be encouraged – BUT ONLY IN THE RIGHT PLACE AND ON THE RIGHT OCCASION. The maintenance of strict secrecy is the responsibility of each individual. A few careless words by one man will jeopardise our enterprise and hazard unnecessarily our lives. Learn the following simple orders; obey them to the letter, AND SEE THAT OTHERS DO LIKEWISE.

SECRECY ORDERS

1. Don't discuss matters of naval or military importance with ANYONE IN ANY OTHER UNIT – whether in the canteen or elsewhere in the camp.

2. Don't discuss important matters with anyone in public places of amusement, such as cafes, restaurants, bars or brothels.

3. When talking in the Officers', or Sergeants' Messes, or in your tents see that the servants ARE NOT LISTENING. They have long ears and understand English better than they can speak it. Send them all (including the barman) outside. DON'T TRUST ANY OF THEM.

4. Don't boast to women. We can boast when our operation has reached a successful conclusion.

REMEMBER THAT

1. Egypt is a neutral country, and the Japanese Embassy is still in residence.

2. From Geneifa to Cairo by road is a short distance. From Cairo to Rome or Berlin by radio wireless is shorter still. This is a plain fact – not an alarming threat.[9]

On the 7 April the situation in Cyrenaica turned disastrous; with the British in retreat German forces captured General O'Connor and much of his command structure in Darnah. Meanwhile, in Genefia a Warning Order was received at around 1500hrs followed by embarkation orders two hours later. Within ten hours of being issued the order, and in a state of anticipation, the commandos packed up their equipment, marched out of the tented camp and were all aboard HMS Glenearn by 0430hrs the following morning. The remainder of that day was spent loading additional store and equipment including explosives and ammunition. At 0730hrs of the 9 April the Glenearn and its cargo of 500 commandos set sail for Ismailia, where it anchored for approximately three hours before arriving in Port Said at 1830hrs.[10] With continued rumours of raids, and the issue of sailing orders at mid day on the 13th many believed that they were about to see action at last. In a strong wind which caused the ship to roll heavily they set sail for Alexandria just after dusk arriving without incident at 0930 hrs the following morning.

Later that day Colonel Laycock attended a conference on HMS Warspite where it was decided that 'A' and 'C' Battalions would carry out a raid on the enemy-held seaport of Bardia and that four Troops from 'B' Battalion would carry out a raid on the coast road near Bomba. Aboard the Glenearn, despite no official notification, excitement among the commandos was mounting, however the realisation that at last they were about to take the fight to the enemy brought with it its own concerns and anxieties; last minute confusion about embarkation drills resulted in a full scale exercise at 1630hrs followed by a second at 1915hrs; and just to add to the tension during the exercise one of the Landing Craft broke loose resulting in one man injured and one Light Machine Gun lost overboard.[11]

With the exercises over by 2000hrs Dick Pedder carried out a number of conferences and lectures with his officers detailing the events for the following day, which would start with a route march around Alexandria. By 0845hrs on the 15 April the commandos had disembarked from the Glenearn before carrying out a two and a half hour march around Alexandria's dock and slum areas. Back on board by 1115hrs they continued with preparations for the pending raid which included the loading of ammunition and on receipt on news of the operation at 1900hrs, more lectures before Dick Pedder issued a detailed administration Warning Order to his officers at 2115hrs:

WARNING ORDER - ADMINISTRATION

Steel helmets, K.D. shirts and battledress trousers with braces, not belts, were to be worn; pockets were to be filled in accordance with Standing Orders. They were to wear rope-soled boots and if they did not have them they were to wear a stout pair of gym shoes, with puttees to be worn in either case. No haversacks were to be used however water bottles were to be filled and whistles and knifes were to be on lanyards under their equipment; wire cutters were to be carried by all. All officers, Warrant Officers (WO's), Sub-Section Leaders, Sgt Hill and L/Cpl Wakefield, were to be in possession of an accurate watch. All in possession of torches will hand them into their Troop Leaders where they will be stacked by Troops in the room detailed by the Regimental Sergeant Major (RSM), before being painted green. Cpl Emms and Tpr Turner, the armourer was to obtain the paint and if no brushes were available they were to use cotton wool. All flasks were to be handed in by Troops to Cpl Mitchell in the room detailed by the RSM, where they will be filled under 2nd Lt Parnacott's supervision. Troops will obtain a supply of corks that will be burnt ready for use. All Cooks and employed men will be withdrawn from the Cookhouse for the purpose of drawing ammunition.

One box of grenades per Sub-Section were to be primed in the Liaison Office on the Poop Deck under the supervision of 2nd Lts Fraser and Ravenscroft, with each primed box chalked with Troop, Section and Sub-Section. Bren - Light Machine Guns (LMG) were to have 12 loaded magazines per gun, with each magazine loaded with one round tracer to one round ball. Magazines were to be loaded in the hold under the supervision of the Artificer Quarter Master Sergeant (AQMS). Thompson (Tommy) machine guns magazines and drums were also to be loaded in the hold, with one drum and five magazines filled. Troops were to carryout loading and priming in the order: 6,7,8,9,10,1,2,3,4,5 with relieved Troop Leaders warning the relieved 10 minutes before. Bren and Tommy guns were loaded simultaneously and no Troop was to enter the hold until the previous Troop had completed its operation. A final amendment stated that as battledress blouses were being worn, shirts Angola, would not; that respirator would not be carried; eye-shields were to be carried in the left pocket of the battledress blouse and that water-wings were to be worn under the battledress with the tube inside, pointing upwards. Finally officers were permitted to wear bonnets in lieu of steel helmets and if they were wearing kilts regimental badges were to be removed from their headdress.[12]

Later that evening at approximately 2200hrs HMS Decoy, with four Troops from 'B' Battalion and Brigade HQ aboard set sail for Bardia followed at 0400hrs on the morning of 16 April by 'A' Battalion aboard the Glengyle, and 'C' Battalion on the Glenearn.[13] Later that morning and in calm water Troop Leaders aboard the Glenearn issued orders before kit and equipment inspections were carried out. As final preparations for the raid continued, including the preparation of demolition charges and the allotment of the following ammunition: Officers – three full magazines, a total of 21 rounds; RSM – Tommy gun with one drum of 50 rounds and five full magazines, a total of 150 rounds; Tommy gunners – 150 rounds of .45; Machine gunners, No1 – 150 rounds, No's 2 and 3 – 160 rounds each; Bomber Parties – 12 grenades in total; and Rifle Parties – 110 rounds per each man. [14]

Throughout the afternoon, and as the easterly wind increased from Force 2 to Force 5, air raid warnings were frequently raised and on one occasion an escorting vessel opened fire on an enemy reconnaissance plane.[15] By 1945 hrs the swell was such that it was clear that there would be surf on the beaches of the proposed landing sites; this was soon confirmed by signals from the submarine Commander, Lieutenant Commander W.J.W Woods, aboard HMS Triumph that the folbots could not leave the submarine.

With HMS Decoy in a similar situation; and with grave concerns, not only with the landing but with what was potentially going to be an extremely hazardous re-embarkation, the Senior Naval Officers, Captain Petrie on the Glengyle and Captain McGregor on the Decoy, cancelled their respective landings at 2000hrs. To the immense disappointment of all involved the expedition returned to Alexandria, arriving just after midday on the 17 April. The following day amongst speculation that the operation would still be carried out, Bob Laycock was informed by GHQ Middle East of their desire that the raid on Bardia should take place. However it was decided that the operation should be carried out by Brigade HQ and 'A' Battalion only. To the commandos of Dick Pedder's 'C' Battalion this was another devastating blow.

As 'A' Battalion and the Glengyle set of to raid Bardia, the disappointed unit remained in Alexandria aboard the Glenearn. On 19 April, after a pay issue and deck inspection by Pedder, they were granted 48 hours shore leave, disembarking on 21 April.

With news that the unit was to move by train from Alexandria to No.3 Transit Camp at Amiriya all the stores and equipment that had been unloaded from the Glenearn were then reloaded on to the train. At 1230 hrs on 22 April they set off by train, arriving two hours later, upon which they marched into what George More described as a comfortable looking Transit Camp.

On 24 April Laycock informed Pedder that 'C' Battalion were being deployed to Cyprus to carryout Garrison duties before being used independently for up and coming operations in Syria; it was on that same day the unit resumed its original title: No.11 (Scottish) Commando. After marching out of the Transit Camp at 1300hrs on 26 April, they boarded a train which carried them to Kantara, where they crossed the Canal to Kantara East on the 0430hrs ferry. From Kantara East they boarded another train and headed for Palestine, crossing the frontier at 0930hrs on 27 April, passing through Gaza and Ladds before finally reaching Haifa at 1730hrs were they went into bivouacs at the IPC Sports Ground for the night. The next day, after breakfast which was cooked for them by the Essex Regiment, they embarked on the S.S.Warzawa and set sail for Cyprus at 1600 hrs on the 29 April.[16]

CHAPTER 4
CYPRUS

April – June 1941

Sailing at a speed of 6 knots, on a calm sea with a slight swell, the Warzawa docked in Famagusta at 1500hrs on 30 April. Unloading commenced an hour later while Geoffrey Keyes, who by now was Second-in-Command of the unit, went on ahead to prepare camp near the town of Salamis. As the commandos were disembarking in Cyprus the situation for the Allies in other parts of the region were becoming increasing bleak. Despite being unable to capture the crucial forward seaport of Tobruk from the besieged British garrison and having to rely on a logistical supply line that ran all the way back to Tripoli, Rommel's Afrika Korps was still dominant in the deserts of North Africa. In the Balkan's the Germans had rampaged through Yugoslavia before sweeping into Greece, forcing Lieutenant General Henry Maitlaind 'Jumbo' Wilson's force of British, Australian, and New Zealanders to rapidly retreat south before finally deciding to evacuate on 21 April. In a repeat of the scenes at Dunkirk valuable heavy equipment and vehicles were abandoned as the troops were evacuated from the beaches. With indications that Hitler would continue south and invade Crete and with the possibility that an invasion of Cyprus was feasible, defences on the island were increased. For the purpose of decentralising responsibility, Cyprus was divided into five Military Areas, 11 (Scottish) Commando were designated Area 'A' which was in the eastern portion of the Island.[1]

The adjutant, George More, drafted provisional measures for the Commando's participation in the defence of the island. Each Troop was designated a location throughout Area 'A' for which it would be responsible for, for a given period of time, the table below shows the designated areas and where and when the Troops were there:

Place.	Dates and Troops.						
	1/5/41	6/5/41	23/5/41	27/5/41	31/5/41	1/6/41	2/6/41
SALAMIS	9,4,10	9,4	9,4	9,4	9,10	5,10	1,10
FAMAGUSTA	2,3	2,3	2,3	2,3	2,3	2,3	2,3
BOGHAZ	-	10	10	-	-	-	-
LEFKONIKO	8	8	-	-	-	-	-
PRASTIO	5	5	5	5	5	9	9
HILEA	-	-	-	10	4	4	4
KONDEA	7	7	-	-	-	-	-
AKHYRITOU	-	-	7,8	7,8	7,8	7,8	7,8
LARNACA	1,6	1,6	1,6	1,6	1,6	1,6	5,6

From the George Hotel on 2 May, Dick Pedder issued his orders, as No. 2 and No.3 Troop moved into the fortress at Famagusta. The following day the remaining Troops marched out to various points in the area to take up defensive positions. No.5 Troop was deployed to Prastio in the Limassol district; Paddy Mayne's No.7 Troop marched out to Kondea; and Captain Ian Glennie's No.8 Troop was dispatched to Lefkoniko. Nos. 4, 9 and 10 Troops were stationed at the ancient city-state of Salamis, 6km north of Farmagusta. However, Tommy Macpherson recalls how his interest in the Ancient Classics resulted in him and some of No.10 Troop being deployed to Yialousa, in the far north-east of the island:

The Commando was fairly broken up there due to the nature of covering the ground and so on, and it happened that I had been studying the Classics and had a Greek background and I backed this up in Cyprus with a few lessons in Modern Greek, and on that very unsound basis I was considered the only Greek speaker in the Commando, so I was sent with my Troop to the north-east corner of the island.[2]

Gerald Bryan's No.1 Troop was stationed in Larnaca where they hired a local gentleman to do the catering:

We were fed extremely well for one shilling a day and alcohol was equally cheap so much so that the men found that for the cost of a pint of beer at home the could buy a bottle of brandy in Cyprus! The results were disastrous until the men realised that although the costs were the same, the effects of one bottle of brandy were somewhat different to a single pint of beer! recalls Bryan.[3]

With the Troop's settled into their new surroundings daily routines and mundane garrison duties soon became the norm, and to some of the men the war that was raging around them at times seemed a million miles away. Time was set aside for recreation activities such as swimming, sailing and horse riding; and from their base in the north of the island, No.10 Troop's, Lance Corporal Davie Rutherford, a Cameron Highlander from Leith, would play his guitar over the field telephones which could be heard all over the island until the headquarters found out! No.8 Troop's Jim Bogle, a Gordon Highlander who had joined the Commando at Brechin, thought, 'That Cyprus was more like a holiday at times.'[4]

However, the good life was not what these men had volunteered for, and the lack of action and the frustration that the war was going on all around them started to take its toll on some, especially when fuelled with cheap and easy to obtain alcohol. Tommy Macpherson remembers how the frustration affected Paddy Mayne:

Paddy Mayne began to get a little excitable, he had not been an enormously heavy drinker before, but perhaps a mixture perhaps of boredom and the Cyprus wine – at a shilling a bottle or something – certainly tempted him. And when he was in his cups he really was extremely difficult to deal with; he was so prodigiously strong and headstrong as well. He would just get an idea into his head, however eccentric, and go ahead and do it. And Eoin McGonigal used to be in the forefront of trying to restrain him but to very little avail. I remember one particular incident, in a nightclub in Nicosia (I wasn't present but I was involved in the upshot), where he and Eoin were that last to leave and he reckoned, probably correctly, that he had been heavily gypped in his bill. So he summoned the manager and the manager proceeded, unwisely, to be rather rude to him. So he forcibly stood the manager in the middle of the wooden floor and emptied the revolver in to the floor around his feet. As a result of it he was arrested and I was his supervising officer.[5]

On 22 May George More issued a Warning Order for the change over of Troops in the detached stations. Detailing that all Troop Leaders must complete all tactical arrangements in their present positions and that they each should prepare a sketch detailing the locations of cached ammunition, food and other such supplies. He emphasised that it was the Troop Leaders responsibility to make arrangements to visit one and others locations so as to personally inspect the ground and location of caches. As the Troops changed locations all camp stores, including tents, blankets and reserve ammunition were left behind for the incoming Troop, the outgoing Troop would march to its new location during the night, each man carrying his own equipment and haversacks, his personal weapon complete with Bardia-scale ammunition. Magazines were ordered to be full; however no man was to carry any grenades. Each Troop was accompanied by the Troop truck which carried equipment including the remaining Bren-guns, tommy-guns, anti-tank rifle magazines and gun boxes. Grenades were left behind fully primed and handed over to the incoming Troop, which was met by a rear party of an officer and one other rank.

Two days prior to More's Warning Order, Hitler decided to continue his Balkan campaign by capturing Crete, which he had feared would be used as a naval and bomber base by the British. The Airborne invasion began on 20 May with glider and parachute landings, the defending British garrison, commanded by the New Zealand First World War hero, Lieutenant-General Bernard Freyberg VC, consisted mainly of lightly armed troops who had just escaped from Greece. After a week of bitter fighting Freyberg ordered a retreat and evacuation.[6] 'A' Battalion of Layforce, fresh from the fiasco of Bardia, and "D" Battalion, the amalgamated Nos. 50 and 52 Middle East Commandos, were sent to Crete to assist with the withdrawal and evacuation of the island. Despite being lightly equipped and armed only with weapons suitable for offensive, close quarter fighting, they were tasked to hold the beach-head while the main forces withdrew through it.[7] As the commandos leapfrogged back from one rearguard position to another they suffered heavy casualties: of the 1200 men who were sent to Crete, about 800 were lost.[8]

With the fall of Crete, and an invasion of Cyprus looking imminent, the Commando was put on invasion alert,[9] and preparation of defensive positions and digging of slit trenches continued around island; men who had served in the Royal Engineers made anti-personnel mines from five inch cast iron piping stuffed with plastic explosive, which were positioned along the sea front and fitted with trip wires; strategic points on the island's road system were mined using the engineer's camouflet equipment; buildings that impeded arcs of fire in strategic positions were prepared for demolition, including the local inland revenue office in Famagusta; and all the while sections carried out patrols and reconnoitred the terrain within their areas.[10]

Germany's stranglehold in the Balkans, North Africa and the Mediterranean had not gone unnoticed elsewhere in the region; in the Middle East, pro-Axis elements in Iraq encouraged a coup that brought the Arab nationalist, Rashid Ali el Gaylani, to power. Rashid Ali hoped that a German victory would liberate the country and the Arabs from the yoke of British control and restrict the growing Jewish presence in Palestine. Encouraged by the Germans, he refused the British their treaty right to transport troops through Iraq and surrounded the airfield at Hibbaniya. Fearful for their lines of communication with India and the supplies of Iraqi oil, the 10th Indian Division landed in Basra, and despite the support of German aircraft flown via Syria, the Vichy French ruled territory, the Iraqis and Baghdad were captured by 31 May 1941. After the French-German Armistice, signed at Compiègne in June 1940, the Free French commanded by General de Gaulle had supported the British. Vichy France however, in the Unoccupied Zone in the south of the country, was a pro-German, anti-British regime, which was at best neutral in the early years of the war.[11] Vichy, under Marshal Philippe Petain, also ruled the French colonies overseas most notably in North Africa with 250,000 troops under the command of General Maxime Weygand, and in the French Mandate of Syria and Lebanon with 45,000 troops under the command of General Henri Dentz.

On the 31 May, Dick Pedder, George More and Captain Richard Carr received urgent orders to proceed by air to Palestine. The following day the trio left Nicosia airport at 0710hrs arriving in Palestine at 0930hrs where they stayed until 1300hrs before travelling to Jerusalem by car, arriving ninety minutes later. After reporting to Palestine Force HQ they checked into their hotels before attending a conference at 1800hrs, where Pedder was briefed by the Commander of the Australian 21 Infantry Brigade on the part that the Commando was to play in the forthcoming operation.[12] On the 3 June while Pedder was still in Palestine, a coded message was sent to the Commando in Cyprus, ordering them to prepare to embark on two destroyers at Famagusta at 0300hrs on the 4 June. The realisation that they were about to escape from the tedium of garrison duties, and at last participate in some action, was not lost on the men back in Cyprus. On receipt of the news Captain Robin Farmiloe burst into a café where some of the officers were having tea and shouted at them to get their men ready to embark within four hours. Troops still deployed at their detachments were brought in on civilian buses commandeered especially for that purpose. Pedder had instructed that equipment and ammunition should be issued as per the Bardia Scale. Assembled at the quay from 0100hrs on the morning of 4 June the commandos, trying to grab some sleep where ever they could, waited impatiently for the two destroyers to dock in the port. Eventual at 0540hrs, and just back from the evacuation of Crete,

Litani River

the bombed and battered Destroyers Rex and Hotspur were docked and ready to start embarking. By 0625hrs, after Captain Farmiloe had ensured that all 25 officers and 431 other ranks were aboard; the officers and men of No.11 (Scottish) Commando under the command of Geoffrey Keyes left the shores of Cyprus.

CHAPTER 5
ACTION AT LAST!

June 1941

As the rear party, consisting of some HQ staff and No.5 Troop under Major Charles Napier a Gordon Highlander, remained in Cyprus to strike the tents in the detachment camps and re-erect them in Salamis, the destroyers Rex and Hotspur were steaming towards Port Said at 25 knots, arriving at 1700hrs on 4 June. Dick Pedder, meanwhile, was in Nazareth attending a conference with General Wilson, the General Officer Commanding (GOC) Palestine, where final details of the forthcoming operation were discussed by all forces and services involved and dates and times were fixed. Later that afternoon Pedder, More and Carr left for Port Said by car, arriving at 0500hrs the following morning.[1] The GOC's Conference concerned the decision to invade Vichy French controlled Syria, which was already being used as a base by the German Air Force.[2] The assistance given by the Vichy French to German aeroplanes using Syria as a staging post on their way to support Rashid Ali's revolt in Iraq, coupled with intelligence gained from Ultra that General Dentz had supplied weapons to the Iraqis,[3] caused Churchill to instruct the Commander-in-Chief Middle East, General Archibald Wavell, to invade and occupy Syria and Lebanon.[4] Incensed by the revelations that the French had freely cooperated with the Germans, and concerned over the threat of German success spreading to the Middle East or the British base in Egypt, had convinced Churchill of the necessity to invade. The Prime Minister would later elaborate to the House of Commons his decision to attack the

Vichy Forces:

It did not take much intelligence to see that the infiltration into Syria by the Germans, and their intrigues in Iraq, constituted very great dangers to the whole Eastern flank in our defence in the Nile Valley and the Suez Canal. The only choice before us in the theatre for some time has been whether to encourage the Free French to attempt a counter-penetration by themselves or, at heavy risk in delay, to prepare, as we have done, a considerable force of our own. It was also necessary to restore the position in Iraq before any serious advance in Syria could be made. Our relations with the Vichy Government and the possibilities of an open breach with it evidently raised the military and strategic significance of these movements to the very highest point. Finally, and above all, the formidable menace of the invasion of Egypt by the German Army in Cyrenaica, supported by large Italian forces with German stiffening, remains our chief preoccupation in the Middle East.[5]

Initial orders for Operation Exporter, the invasion of Vichy French controlled Syria and Lebanon, were issued on 5 June by HQ Palestine Force. The aim of the invasion and subsequent occupation was to prevent the establishment of a German presence there that could threaten Britain's bases in Palestine and its broader strategic position in the eastern Mediterranean. The operation was also timed to take advantage of losses suffered by German forces during their invasion of Crete.[6] However, the hastiness of the operation was apparent from the beginning; ten days before the proposed start date General Wilson was still unable to tell the divisional commander exactly what units would be in his force; and only a few copies of an Intelligence handbook providing information about the Syrian roads, towns and people and the defending army were available.[7] The invading force was quickly drawn together from available forces which included the 7th Australian Division under the command of Major-General John Lavarack, less the 18th Brigade which was involved at the Siege of Tobruk; the 5th Indian Infantry Brigade Group commanded by Brigadier Wilfrid Lewis Lloyd; and the 1st Free French Division commanded by Major-General Paul Louis Le Gentilhomme. Wilson's initial plan involved a simultaneous three-pronged advance from Palestine. Lavarack's 7th Division was ordered to march by two main routes and subdivide his force into two further groups: Left Group and Right Group. Left Group consisted of the 21st Australian Infantry Brigade and attached troops, including Dick Pedder's Commando. Left Group, less Pedder's men, was to advance north along the coast through the ancient cities of Tyre and Sidon, with Beirut as its objective. Right Group consisting of 25th Australian Infantry Brigade was detailed to advance north along an inland route, to the east of the 21st Brigade, with its objective the major Vichy French airbase at Rayak. The third prong of the advance was to take place further inland to the east, where the 5th Indian Brigade followed by the 1st Free French Force was ordered to advance to Damascus. The initial objective of the 21st Infantry Brigade, under the command of Brigadier Stevens, was to cross the frontier at approximately 0200hrs on the morning of 8 June and to advance to and capture the coastal city of Tyre. For this phase of the operation Stevens divided his force into two main columns: "DONCOL" consisting of the 2/16th Infantry Battalion under Lt. Col. A.B. MacDonald; and "MOTCOL" consisting of Lt. Col. M.J. Moten's 2/27th Infantry Battalion;[8] two further columns included in the 21st Brigade's Order of Battle comprised of the horse-mounted Cheshire Yeomanry, and the Australian 2/14th Battalion who were detailed with specialist and reserve roles.⁹ Stevens, who had served in France in the previous war, was short and slight in stature, but waspishly aggressive and persistent in action.¹⁰ He had been hand picked by Lavarack in 1940 and given the task of forming and commanding the 21st Brigade. For the first phase of the operation Stevens's sector ran from the sea at Ras en Naqoura eastwards for 25-miles following a line of lofty, rugged hills into which the only entrance for motor vehicles was the coast road. Steven's problem in the coastal sector was also greatly complicated by the likelihood that the defenders would demolish the roads and bridges ahead of him; particularly the road a few miles north of Ras en Naqoura, and the Qasmiye Bridge over the Litani River. The enemy was known to be holding the line of the Litani River, which runs south before turning west into the Mediterranean. The Commando's task was to co-ordinate with the 21st Brigade's attack on the river position by carrying out an amphibious assault landing from the sea near to the mouth of the river. Once ashore their task was to secure the north and south banks of the river, and prevent the demolition of the Qasmiye Bridge that crossed it, allowing Steven's Brigade to advance towards Beirut engaging the enemy in the process. The advancing forces were to be supported by gunfire from naval vessels offshore, including the anti-aircraft cruiser HMS Coventry and the destroyers Ilex, Isis, Hotspur and Hero. Air support was provided a number of air force squadrons including No.11 Squadron RAF, No. 80 Squadron RAF, No. 208 Squadron RAF (Army Co-operation), X Flight RAF and No.3 Squadron RAAF.

The Commando embarked in the Glengyle on 6 June, and along with its escorts, the destroyers Hotspur, Ilex and Hero, set sail from Port Said at 1200hrs the following day.¹¹ However, intelligence had not been supplied as to the beach landing sites involved, nor were they included in the RAF aerial photographs of the coast. The only maps available were on a scale of 1 to 200,000, whereas maps on a scale of 1 to 25,000 or 50,000 would have been more advantageous. This lack of intelligence caused the Senior Naval Officer (SNO) to send his Senior Beach Master, Lieutenant Potter, RN to Haifa in HMS Hero, to obtain information on the landing site. Aboard the motor-boat Gadwell, Lt Potter and Sub-Lt F.H. Colenut, RNR, carried out a reconnaissance of the coast in the early hours of 7 June. This reconnaissance showed that heavy surf was running at an average distance of 300 yards from the beach as a result of ground swell, and that during the next two days the prospect of landing without considerable loss was not good. It was however, decided to make an attempt the following morning, 8 June.[12]

CHAPTER 6
FARCICAL BEGINNINGS

8 June 1941

The Glengyle arrived at a point four miles west of the mouth of the Litani River at 0038hrs on 8 June, eleven Amphibious Landing Craft (ALC) were lowered into the water with the commandos packed into them. As the last of the men were boarding the craft, Potter and Colenut arrived alongside in the Gadwall. Potter expressed that in his opinion the surf was so bad that the flat bottomed landing craft would roll over if they attempted to make a beaching. This view was also shared by Colenut, who was an Inspector in the Sea Section of the Palestine Police, and who like Potter, had considerable experience of the coast. The Senior Naval Officer (SNO) had delegated overall responsibility as to whether the boats could be beached or not, to Captain Petrie RN of the Glengyle. After listening to the concerns of Potter and Colenut, Petrie decided that because the ALCs that were being used were not suitable to be used in surf and would capsize before reaching the beach, the operation could not be undertaken.[1] This view was not shared by Dick Pedder who argued that the risk was worth taking in order to maintain the element of surprise, especially as the Glengyle was visible in the moonlight and that the enemy would be aware of its presence. Nevertheless, Petrie had over all control of the situation, and no sooner had the men got settled into the ALCs than they were given the order to disembark. With some difficulty, due to the ship moving around in the swell, the craft were re-hoisted back on the Glengyle. With all safely embarked the ship and its cargo of disgruntled commandos set sail back to Port Said. Arriving at 1500hrs later that day, the men stayed on board while Pedder and More went straight to a conference aboard HMS Rex. Within an hour they were back on board and the operation was back on. To the disbelief of most on board, the Glengyle set sail once at 1615hrs. As the Glengyle headed for Syria, Dick Pedder issued his revised orders for the operation, which were as follows:

Précis of Orders by Lt-Col R.R.N. Pedder H.L.I.[2]

ORDERS

INFORMATION

The enemy, approximate strength two battalions of native troops held the position to the north of the Litani River. The river was covered by small arms fire from concrete posts along the hillside. The main bridge across the river was probably destroyed. The 21st Australian Infantry Brigade was attempting to cross the river. A rapid passage with only slight casualties was vital to the success of the whole operation. They had artillery support and there was a squadron of armoured cars with them.

INTENTION

The Bn. would seize and hold enemy positions long enough for the Australian Brigade to cross the river and pass through the position.

METHOD

The Bn. was to land from H.M.S. GLENGYLE at dawn and attack the enemy position from the flank. For this purpose three parties were formed and ALCs were allotted to them.

"X" Party – Commander: Major G.C.T. KEYES
Troops: 2, 3, 9. ALCs: 4

"Y" Party – Commander: Lt-Col R.R.N. PEDDER
Troops: 1, 7, 8. ALCs: 4

"Z" Party – Commander: Capt. G.R.M.H. More

Troops: 4, 10. ALCs: 3

No. 6 Troop were left on board as the ALCs could only be lightly loaded

Forward Troops would be "X" Party

Reserve Troops would be "Y" Party

"Z" Party was an additional reserve, with a main role of preventing enemy reinforcements and supplies reaching their positions.

ADMINISTRATION

Medical Orderlies were attached to each Party.

One No.18 Set accompanied each party, also a No.11 Set with "Z" Party.

The No.11 Set would get in touch with the Australians.

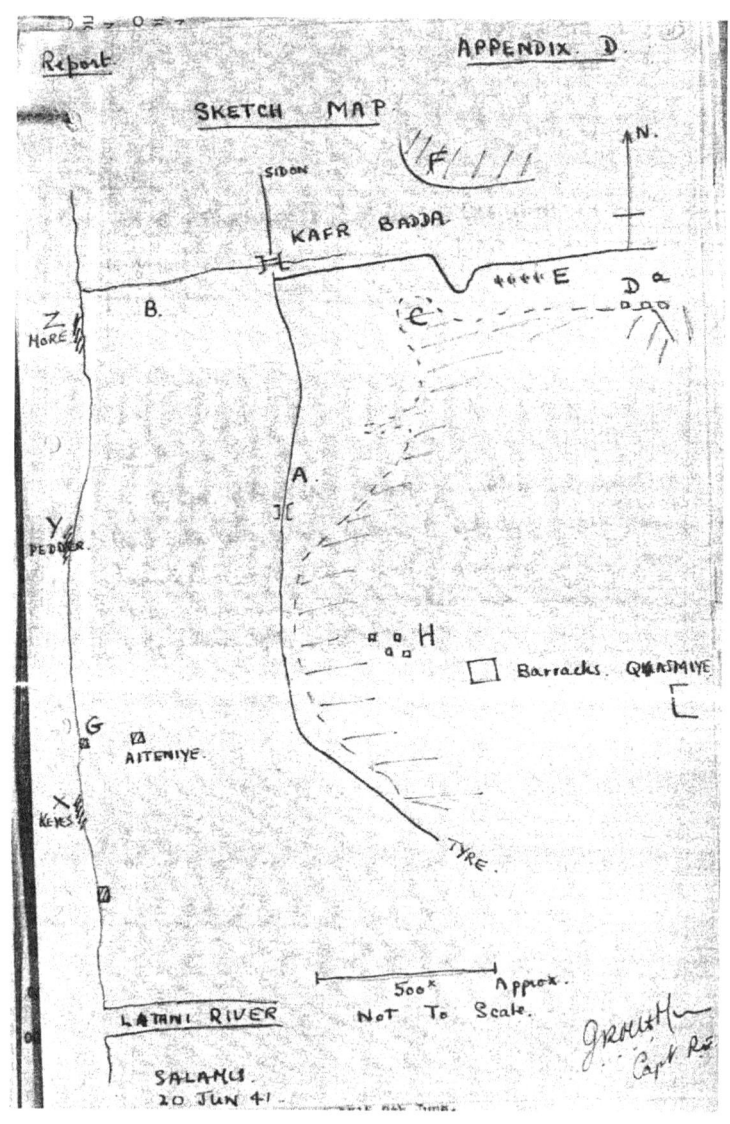

George More's Sketch Map showing landing sites

Photo courtesy of War Diary PRO 218/171

Meanwhile, as the frustrated commandos were re-embarking back on to the Glengyle in the early hours of the morning of 8 June the Australian advance was well under way. At 2130hrs on the previous night, two small parties of rubber-shod men of the 2/14th Battalion and 2/6th Field Company crossed the frontier; one, led by Captain Gowling, intent on cutting lines of communication between the frontier post at Ras en Naqoura to the post at the point in the coastal road near Iskandaroun, where the French had placed demolition charges; and the other under led by Lt. Kyffin, tasked to advance to the demolition site, overcome the guards, and remove the charges.[3] At around 0330hrs, and after covering about 15 miles, Kyffin's party reached the road just north of the point near Ras el Bayada where they had been told the charges were. In the darkness, they examined various bridges and culverts and found that they were not mined. At about 0500hrs when they were north of Iskandaroun, the party was fired on from a strong-post built of stone. The Australians rushed the post and took it; a long, grim fight began which attracted one group after another of French reinforcements. Around 0700hrs a loud explosion was heard south along the road; and the Australians guessed that the road had been blown somewhere on the cliff face north of Naqoura. The demolition they had tried to prevent had been carried out. Although they had been wrongly informed that the road was mined north not south of Iskandaroun, and had failed to prevent the demolition, the party had succeeded in clearing the road for some distance north of the demolition and had captured some thirty prisoners, a number of weapons, six vehicles including one armoured car, and more than thirty horses abandoned by African cavalrymen.[4]

Despite only receiving one casualty it was already

clear to the invading force that the French were there to fight hard and offer more than a half hearted resistance that had been earlier anticipated; in an Intelligence Summary based on information received on 01 June, and issued on 02 June a note on French troops in Syria detailed that:

The attitude of the French troops is very uncertain and it is possible that in some instances French troops will surrender without fighting. Naturally they will surrender more readily if our force shows its determination to overcome quickly any resistance which may be offered. Whilst showing this determination an opportunity should be given them to surrender. If the "Olive Branch" is rejected, the best course will be to strike hard and strike quickly.[5]

However with six regiments of regular soldiers in the region; including Foreign Legion, mixed Colonial and Metropolitan, and African natives, the French were well manned. With around 9000 horse and motorised cavalry, and ninety field and medium guns to call on, evidence was mounting that the French troops in Syria would resist; and that the first serious battle would be encountered north of the Litani River where it had been reported that at least one battalion of Algerians were occupying well fortified defensive positions.[6]

With 21 Brigade pouring into Tyr from the south and the east, the city eventually surrendered just after 1700hrs on 8 June. Brigadier Stevens and the Brigade Command entered the city at 1800hrs and immediately proclaimed martial law. However the passage along the coast had not been without incident; the high ground on the east which ran west down towards the coast had provided excellent defensive positions for the retreating enemy, causing the Australian Brigade to fight the whole way. Meanwhile engineers working on the demolished coastal road had made the road passable to motor transport by 2000hrs and an hour later the Brigade HQ had moved into position just south of Tyr.

By that stage Stevens knew that the Commando had been unable to land from the sea, and that a second attempt would be made the following morning, he issued orders that if his own troops crossed the Litani River before 0400hrs on 9 June they were to fire four verey lights to warn the commandos not to land. If no lights were seen, Stevens informed his Brigade that the Commando would be coming ashore at 0430hrs with orders to establish a bridgehead near the Qasmiye Bridge which had been destroyed by the enemy as they withdrew over the river.[7]

Stevens also ordered that if the Commando was unsuccessful Lt Col MacDonald's 2/16th Battalion was to commence an attack at 0530hrs with the intention of attacking and capturing Barrack Ridge, on the north side of the river. In the event of the Commando's objective not being completed, MacDonald allotted the task of establishing a bridgehead near to the point that the bridge was blown, to 'A' Company to which a fourth platoon was attached to carry canvas boats forward in case they were needed. 'B' Company was detailed to cover the operation from the high ground to the right. 'C' Company were to cross the river in all available assault boats and 'D' Company were to supply the carrying parties.[8]

CHAPTER 7
LITANI RIVER – X PARTY

9/10 June 1941

As on the previous evening the Glengyle and its escorts arrived about 4 miles to the west of the mouth of the Litani River, and at just after 0300hrs, in calm weather, with no noticeable surf and in complete darkness, the landing-craft were lowered into the water. With the full moon silhouetting the Glengyle on the horizon, X Party, consisting of Nos. 2, 3, and 9 Troops under the command of Geoffrey Keyes, were formed up in four landing-craft by 0325hrs. Keyes had received orders from Dick Pedder to attack the positions and barracks due east of Aitenyie Farm and hold the enemy on as wide a front as possible.[1] The party set for the shore under the command of the Royal Navy's Lieutenant Collar. With the morning sun due to rise to their fronts Collar had the responsibility of getting the party to the correct landing point on the shore. However, with day break more than an hour away, and a lack of aerial photographs showing the mouth of the river or the coastline, Collar soon experienced difficulties in finding the correct landing site, resulting in the party being landed at 0450hrs, approximately a mile to the south of the desired landing point, and on the wrong side of the river. With only a ground swell to contend with, most of the men managed to get ashore without getting very wet and without incurring any opposition from the French. In his report Lt Collar later detailed the circumstances of the landing from the Navy's perspective:

> No difficulty was experienced in slipping the boats of

this Division, and the first 3 boats to be lowered quickly formed up 1 cable off the starboard bow of the Glengyle, to wait for the ALC from No.7 Davits. During this wait, the other two Divisions moved off around the bow and turned towards the shore. The 3rd Division did not follow until its fourth ALC had left the ship, and therefore formed up rather hurriedly as the flotilla moved off. It was later found that the ALC was in the wrong position, so, at the request of the Military this was corrected on the way in. It was found that the petrol launch leading us in was heading for the small white house which had been made out from the bridge, so the 3rd Division followed it until it turned away about half a mile from the beach. It was thought probable that the river mouth was just South of this house, but during the final approach no signs of the river could be made out, and the 3rd Division finally beached with the Northern ALC just south of the house. A moderate scend was experienced during the last 300 yards, but this did not develop, and except for one small stretch where a sandbar existed, the boats beached without the surf breaking at all. This division was deployed by signal when it was about 500 yards from the beach, as no sign of surf was visible and it was thought that the boats might come on it suddenly from to seaward. Apart from momentary qualms when a cypress grove was mistaken for a platoon of the enemy, no signs of opposition were seen during the landing and the troops cleared the boats in quick time, one officer, perhaps the keenest of all, going up to the tin hat; the remainder were almost all dry from their knees up. Kedges were used when beaching and the loss of three of these was the only damage sustained by the boats in this division. As soon as the troops were clear, all boats at once proceeded to seaward for ½ mile and as soon as the last boat had turned away from the beach, all proceeded at full speed for the destroyers. About 6 minutes after the troops were clear a battery of Field Guns opened fire on the exact sector of beach which had been used, though all boats were well clear and the troops must have been well inland. A few rounds of small arms fire was the only other sign of opposition to this landing. As soon as the field gun battery was located the destroyers opened fire on it and shortly ceased fire. The trip to Haifa was made in company with 3 ALC and 1 SLC without difficulty. It cannot be definitely stated whether the troops were landed to the North or South of the river, as no signs of the river mouth was seen, but by judging by the gully in which the white house was situated, it is now thought probable that the river mouth was to the north of this beech. The abundance of white buildings made comparison with the Army map, on which one was only marked, useless, and owing to the lack of air photos the course of the last ½ mile of the river could not be determined.[2]

Once ashore they advanced to the top of the beach and removed their haversacks. Geoffrey Keyes would later write in his report that:

By then it was light enough to see the masts of the feluccas in the river mouth, and I realised that we were south of the river, I at once issued orders to advance with "A" Section, No. 2 Troop, under Lt T.I. Robinson, Gordon Highlanders, leading, with the river as the first objective. We advanced along the beach, deployed just below the crest and passed through "C" Company, 2/16 Australian Infantry Battalion, who were waiting to support the attack north of the river. The Company Commander was very surprised to see us, but said he would lend me some of his seven boats, which he had moved up with some of his men and with my reserve.[3]

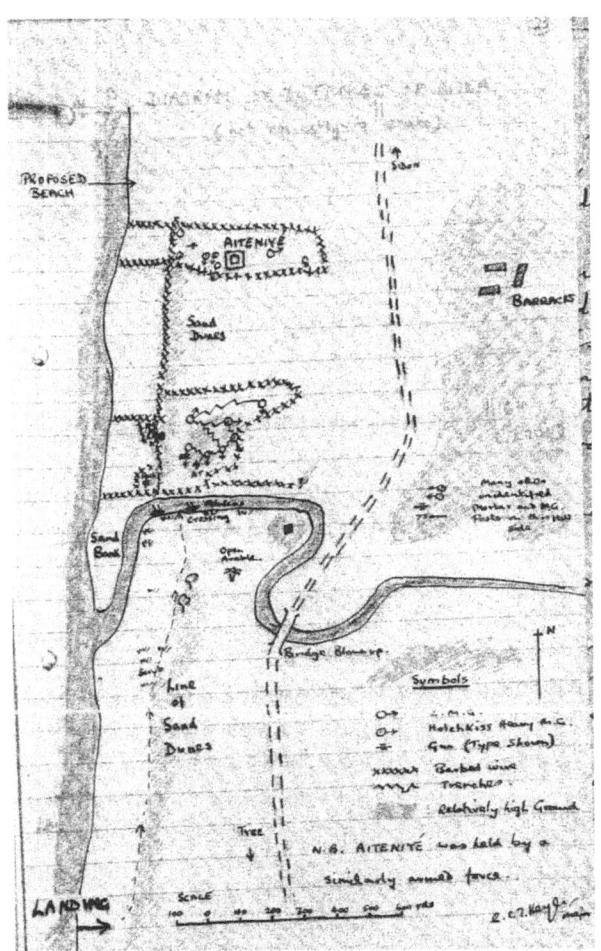

Geoffrey Keyes X Party Sketch Map
Photo courtesy of War Diary PRO 218/171

At about 0510hrs, as the advanced troops reached the river bank, a red Verey light, signalling S.O.S, was fired from a redoubt on the far bank. Immediately the entire beach from where they had landed, right up to within yards of the river came under heavy and sustained fire from 75mm guns, mortars, and heavy machine-guns, from the direction of the main ridge to the north-east. As heavy fire rained down on the party they were pinned to the ground, and several casualties were taken, mainly by accurate sniper fire from a knoll on the opposite bank and from enemy positions to the north. A Section of No.3 Troop under Captain George Highland and Lieutenant Eric Garland succeeded in working forward on the right of No. 2 Troop before getting held up again. The area on the approach to the river from the south side was flat and open ground which offered very little cover for the advancing commandos making progress not only slow but extremely treacherous. Geoffrey Keyes later described the early stages of the operation in his diary:

We all go to ground, as 75 mm guns, 81 mm mortars, and heavy machine-guns all firing very accurately. George Highland, Davidson and self behind substantial bush and low bank. Extremely unpleasant. Davidson moves about thirty yards to right, but gets pinned behind low bush by snipers in wired post on far side of the river. Very accurate fire. Padbury, Jones, Woodnutt killed, Wilkinson badly wounded. George and Eric [Garland] as cool as cucumbers take most of 3 Troop about sixty yards to right flank. Can get no further, as open ground.[4]

Eric Garland

Photo courtesy of
National War Museum Scotland

George Highland

Photo courtesy of
National War Museum Scotland

Around this point, LCpl Dilworth, Pte Arthur, Pte Harris and Pte Archibald from 14 Platoon of C Company, 2/16 AIB started to carry the boat forward which would be used by the commandos to cross the river. Despite encountering heavy mortar, LMG and rifle fire, the four Australians showed great courage in getting the boat to the south bank. Unfortunately during their effort Pte Arthur was killed.[5]

Geoffrey Keyes, who was still using the bush as cover, was hesitant about moving out into the open ground, which was covered by enemy sniper fire, in order to reach George Highland's position. However, despite the risks, Keyes accompanied by Pte Ness, started to crawl towards Davidson's position, an extremely dangerous task that took them about twenty five minutes to cover about thirty yards. On reaching Davidson, Keyes and Ness decided to run across the open ground in front of them. After a few steps Keyes who was heavily laden tripped and fell, with Ness going to ground beside him in a very exposed position, so under continued sniping, Keyes ordered Ness to run to Highland's position, which he did safely. Geoffrey Keyes meanwhile took cover for approximately ten minutes before setting off in two bursts to reach Highland and Ness. On the way he inspected the bodies of 32-year-old Corporal Harold Jones (Royal Armoured Corps) and 28-year-old Sapper Desmond Woodnut (Royal Engineers), and found both men dead. Upon reaching their position he found George Highland and Eric Garland engaged in a high risk method of drawing the sniper's fire, which was inflicting many casualties. Garland, exposing himself to the sniper, drew his fire, and once located, shot him with his Bren gun. Also engaging the enemy was Signaller Reed, who had taken over the gun after his Corporal had been shot, and despite having to withdraw to cover and clean the sand clogged weapon, Reed returned under heavy fire and got involved in the action.⁶

With the sniper taken care off and during a brief lull in the firing Eric Garland, Cpl Southall, Sig Reed, Pte Hughes and three other men from No.3 Troop, climbed into the boat that had been brought forward by LCpl Dilworth and his men from C Company. With the boat positioned out of the line of sight of the redoubt LCpl Dilworth and Pte Archibald coolly ferried the commandos across the fast flowing river, which was approximately 30-40 yards wide, before returning for a second party of troops.⁷ Geoffrey Keyes reported the situation:

No. 3 Troop were still 200 yards from the river until about 0930hrs when our artillery ranged onto the redoubt. This allowed me to move with Capt Highland and Lt Garland, about 20 men of Nos. 2 and 3 Troops, and the boat, to the rushes on the south bank. There seemed to be a lull, and we were out of sight of the redoubt, Lt Garland and 6 of his men, and two Australians got across the river at approx 1000hrs, and the Australians brought back the boat. We were pinned down for one and a half hours by MG fire and what we thought to be mortar fire. Actually it was later found to be a 75mm Gun on the high ground east of the road.⁸

Meanwhile on the north side of the river Eric Garland and his party was patiently cutting through the barbed wire entanglements surrounding the redoubt. Sensing an attack was imminent the enemy soon indicated that they were willing to surrender to the advancing commandos. This action was later reported by Keyes:

Captain Highland and I noticed a white flag waving in the redoubt. In the next lull, Captain Highland and 6 men got across, the same Australians bringing the boat back. Captain Highland then captured the redoubt after a short parley, with the loss of one man shot dead while clearing an isolated post.[9]

With Garland and Highland's party's securing the ground around the redoubt and tentatively taking up positions on the north side of the river, Pte Harris, the third man in Dilworth's party, despite being wounded and under fire, carried messages back and forth between the south bank of the river and the Australians lines.[10] Keyes also sent LCpl Dilworth back to bring up what was left of X Party, members of his own Company and more boats. Despite being under-fire both ways, Dilworth returned after about 20 minutes and reported to Keyes that Capt Johnson commanding No.9 Troop, upon hearing that Major Keyes and all the forward troops had been killed, had withdrawn his troops. Johnson had reformed his men with the intention of attacking with the Australians on the right flank; however, while doing so Johnson had met Brigadier Stevens, who had ordered him to send his men to join the 21st Brigade's, B Echelon. Dilworth also informed Keyes that his own Company Commander, Major Caro, was re-organising and would be moving up in support.[11] Determined to assist X Party in whatever way he could, Dilworth joined the commandos in the attack by arming himself with the rifle belonging to the recently killed Driver Alexander Hamilton of the Royal Signals.[12]

At about 1300hrs and during a lull in the action, the C Company Commander, Major Caro, accompanied by No. 9 Troop's Leader, Capt Johnston, moved up to the river to ascertain what was happening. To their surprise they met Geoffrey Keyes, who showed them Garland and Highland's men clearing the enemy position on the north side. However, despite the success of crossing the river and taking the redoubt, the job was far from done and this was emphasised to Keyes by men from No.2 Troop as they came forward to cross the river. As they approached they informed him that Sgt Burton, LCpl Lang and Cohen were all dead on the river bank to the left, and that several of the Troop were wounded. According to Trooper Norman Wilkinson, who was severely wounded, Ike Cohen the Section first aid man saw that Burton was hit and went to try and help him. Wilkinson later reported that:

Burton told him to, 'Stay where he was,' but not Ike, he crawled over and both were killed together. [13]

Norman Wilkinson

Photo courtesy of
The Wilkinson Collection

In the process of taking the redoubt, six enemy soldiers were killed and thirty-five prisoners were taken, and fearing a counter-attack, Highland did not waste any time in organising the defence of the position. In response to a further urgent message sent by Keyes, C Company's Major Caro came forward to his position. Keyes asked for immediate support, pointing out that the Australians could come up along the shore out of sight of the ridge. However, by failing to use the cover available to them they soon drew heavy fire from the enemy who were positioned on the rising ground to the east. With no significant advance being made by the Australians, Geoffrey Keyes took all his remaining men over the river using the boat, sending it back with the prisoners captured in the redoubt. Efforts to take the enemy position had resulted in considerable casualties for the party. As many of the Bren guns and their crews had been lost on the south bank of the river, Keyes made full use of the weapons captured in the heavily fortified redoubt, as well as at least 3 days hard rations and a much needed spring of fresh water; among the captured weapons and ammunition were a 25mm anti-tank gun and limber; a 37.5mm Pack mountain gun; two heavy Hotchkiss machine guns; six Light machine guns; about forty rifles and several thousand rounds.

Meanwhile about 20 Australians commanded, by Lt O'Keith, crossed the river in support of the commandos. However with each boat drawing the enemy's fire, the Company Commander soon decided that it was too dangerous and stopped any more men from crossing. By about 1330hrs X Party had located the gun that was firing down the river, and using the 25mm anti-tank gun captured in the redoubt, Lt Garland turned it around and fired at the enemy's position, putting the offending gun out of action with only seven rounds. A search of the enemy position the following day showed that it contained a heavy machine gun and a 75mm gun that had been badly damaged.

The Australians continued to cross the river and take up positions around the redoubt, and at 1800 hrs Keyes handed over responsibility for its defence to C Company of the 2/16 Infantry Battalion, the whole of which was across the river by 1900hrs. As he had no orders to move, Keyes decided to keep his men where they were. By this time they had been joined by a few men from Nos.1 and 4 Troops who had lost contact with their Troops. Later that evening at around 2100hrs the Australians moved north to attack the next French position at Aiteniye, and the commandos resumed responsibility for the redoubt. However the Australian attack was unsuccessful, and after some difficult extractions, they soon returned to Keyes' position.

CHAPTER 8
LITANI RIVER – Y PARTY

9/10 June 1941

Y Party, consisting of the Commando HQ, and Nos.1, 7 and 8 Troops, left HMS Glengyle, under the command of Dick Pedder at around 0330hrs on 9 June. The landing craft beached approximately 600 yards north of the Litani River at about 0420hrs, with No.1 Troop landing on the right, No.7 Troop in the centre and No.8 Troop on the left. As soon as the first of the commandos hit the beach the enemy opened fire with mortars, heavy machine guns and rifles from their defensive positions along the coast north of the Litani River. The original task of Y Party had been to act as a reserve for X Party. However by landing to the south of the river, X Party had lost all contact with the rest of the Commando, since radio communications had become impossible from the beginning of the raid - X Party's No.18 Set had got a bullet through it early on, and the No.11 Set, which was the only means of contacting the Australians, was also damaged and out of action early in the operation. Unable to make contact with X Party, the three Troops from Y Party had no option but to operate independently.

Commando HQ and No.1 Troop, led by Lt Alistair Coode, B Section's officer, who was in charge of the Troop in the absence of Capt Richard Carr;[1] accompanied by Commando HQ, they were landed on the beach by landing craft No.1, and as soon as they disembarked from the craft, they came under heavy fire from a point to the south of their position. Gerald Bryan, who was A Section's officer, recalls the frantic landing:

> I raced madly up the beach and threw myself into the cover formed by a sand dune. The men behind me were still scrambling out of the landing craft and dashing over the twenty yards of open beach. Away on the right we could hear the rattle of a machine gun and the overhead whine of bullets, but they seemed fairly high. I was just beside a dry stream bed and so started to walk along it, at the same time trying to untie the lifebelt attached to my rifle. Colonel Pedder was shouting at us to push on as quickly as possible. Soon the ditch that I was in became too narrow and there was nothing for it but to climb out into the open. The ground was flat with no cover. The machine guns were now firing fairly continuously but were not very worrying. When I got out into the open - rather like moorland - I started shouting, "A Section No. 1 Troop," which represented my command. Before long we were in pretty good formation, with myself, batman and tommy gunner in the centre.[2]

RSM Tevendale, a Gordon Highlanders, who landed with the Commando HQ, later in his report described the situation:

> Immediately the boat beached we came under very heavy machine gun, rifle and mortar fire from a point about 300 yards south or right of our landing point which could be detected by the great number of tracer bullets used by the enemy. Immediately the firing started the landing craft made back to sea which resulted in about seventy five percent of the men having to swim ashore or at least wade in water up to the neck. We crawled off the beach and advanced along a dried river bed thus breaking through the enemy's first line of defence without sustaining one casualty. For the first 100 yards of our advance we

came under heavy machine gun fire from the hills about 1200 yards away. This fire was obviously directed towards the beach at random, as the light was not good enough for us to be seen at that distance, we reached the coast road without further incident.[3]

Litani River

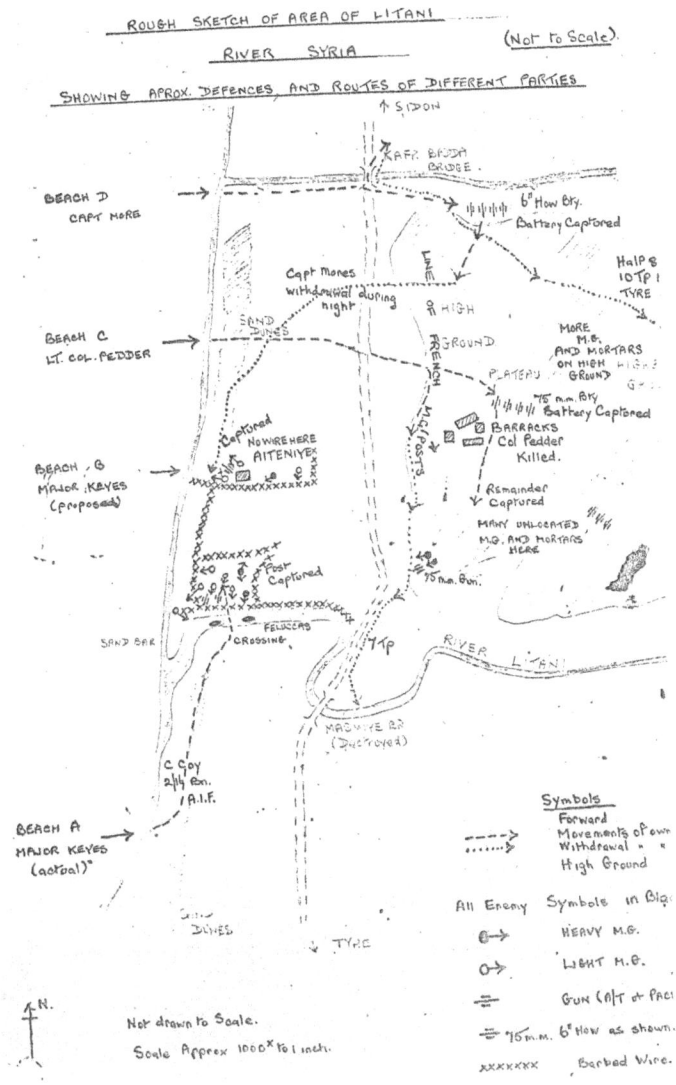

Bill Fraser's Sketch Map showing defensive positions

Photo courtesy of War Diary PRO 218/171

As they advanced towards the coastal road they were aware that the heavy firing from the machine gun posts to their right, which had engaged them as they landed on the beach, had turned their attention towards the troops that had landed to the south, Geoffrey Keyes' X Party. As the enemy had been unable to locate them they did not return fire so as to avoid giving away their position. As they reached the coastal road and started to close in on the enemy, Bryan and his men approached the main road and observed on the other side a trench that stood out clearly in the white chalk. An initial investigation showed that the trench was empty, but behind it his men identified two caves situated within a small cliff face. While his men stood ready with grenades and machine guns, Bryan fired his rifle into the left hand cave, which resulted in seven surprised and sleepy enemy soldiers appearing from the cave wearing only their pyjamas and vests. Bryan left his batman with the captured soldiers with instructions to hand them over to the members of the Commando HQ who were coming up behind them. As Bryan and his section pushed further inland they started to encounter stiffer opposition than that offered by the soldiers in the cave and it was only a matter of time before the section started taking casualties, as Bryan recalled:

It was now quite light, the time being about 0500hrs. The rest of the section had pushed on, so I followed, and came on a wire running along the ground. This I cut with a pair of wire cutters. I found the section held up and under fire from snipers.

As Bryan was deciding on the best course of action for the situation, he was joined by one of his Section corporals who showed him where his water bottle was hit by an enemy bullet. As they discussed his good fortune the corporal was shot in the left eye and killed instantly. As the dead corporal lay at his feet Bryan dived for cover, for he had no idea where the shot had been fired from. Despite the shock of the incident Bryan had no time to dwell on it due to the sudden realisation that some twenty five yards from his position, concealed in the scrub, was a French 75mm gun firing rapidly. Jumping to his feet, Bryan starts to throw grenades at the gun and was quickly followed by others in his Section. To their relief the gun stopped firing, but the fight had been costly and casualties had been taken:

We had three casualties, which wasn't so good. A corporal was shot through the wrist and was cursing every Frenchman ever born. As he couldn't use a rifle, I gave him my Colt automatic pistol, and he carried on.[4]

RSM Tevendale also details his first encounter with the enemy:

When we crossed the coast road the telephone wires were cut also the field communication wires leading from the enemy's forward positions to their French 75mm guns and mortars on the hill beyond their barracks. The advance continued along a deep gully on the north side of the barracks where several prisoners, who were guarding large quantities of explosives and ammunition stored in two separate quarries, were captured. Several of the guards were still in bed and were taken without a shot being fired.[5]

As they reached the barracks they were pinned down by machine gun fire from about 800 yards in an easterly direction to their front and from mortar fire from a point about 300 yards to the north on their left. A short while later Capt Farmiloe commanded a party whose actions put the mortars out of use, causing the enemy to desert the machine gun posts. At about 0700hrs, with the barracks in the hands of the commandos, Dick Pedder ordered Private Adams to enter the barracks and return with the French flag that had been flying there, but unfortunately 22 year old Pte Jack Adams from the Black Watch was killed in action later that day. About 15 minutes after Adams retrieved the flag four 75mm guns opened a heavy barrage onto the beach from about 1000 yards north of the barracks. RSM Tevendale and Capt Farmiloe then moved to the edge of the ridge on the north side of the gully to see what they could learn about the enemy's position and the whereabouts of No.1 Troop. On reaching the ridge they observed a small group of men commanded by Lt Bryan, throw at least three well-directed hand grenades onto the enemy 75mm gun position which they then rushed and captured. On taking the post Bryan's party then turned the captured gun in the direction of the other guns and fired at them, destroying them in the process. Bryan and his men had also been accompanied on this mission by Lt Alistair Coode, who, like Bryan, was a Royal Engineer, and members of his B Section. Bryan recalled the events:

We crawled through some scrub to get closer to the gun. Here we met B Section officer Alastair Coode and a few men also attacking the gun position, so we joined forces. The gun itself was deserted, the crew being in a slit trench. We bunged in a few more grenades and then went in ourselves. It was rather bloody. My section was comprised mostly of Royal Artillery blokes who knew how to handle the gun, and in a few minutes Sgt Worrall, had discovered which fuses to use from one of the original gun crew. This gun was the right hand gun of a battery of four, the others being anything from about 100 yards to 300 yards away. They were still firing. Our gun was pointing away from the battery, so we grabbed the tail piece and heaved it right round so that it was pointing towards the nearest gun. The Sergeant took over command of the gun, shoved a shell in and sighted over open sights, then fired. The result was amazing. There was one hell of an explosion in the other gun site and the gun was flung up into the air like a toy. We must have hit their ammo dump. No time to waste. The Sergeant traversed onto the next gun, sighted rapidly and fired. There was a pause. Where the devil had the shell gone? Then there was a flash and a puff of smoke in the dome of a chapel about half a mile up the hillside. A thick Scottish voice said, "That'll make the buggers pray!" The Sergeant hurriedly lowered the elevation and fired again, this time a bit low. However, the gun crew started to run away and our Bren opened up and did good work. Just then a runner turned up with orders from the Colonel to report to him with as many men as possible when we had finished off the battery. It did not take long to get a good hit on each of the two remaining guns. The Sergeant then broke off the firing pin of our gun with the butt of a rifle.[6]

Bryan duly reported the action of the party to the Commanding Officer and the advance continued.

Earlier No.8 Troop, under the command of Capt Ian Glennie, landed on dry ground around 0420hrs slightly north of their intended landing place, and headed north along the coast for 400 yards without incurring any enemy fire before turning east. As the Troop advanced, contact was lost between B, the forward Section, and A, the reserve Section. It was about this stage that B Section, under Lt Fraser, came into contact with No.7 Troop to their right and ended up supporting it for the early part of the operation. A Section meanwhile moved east away from the beach for about 200 yards before coming under heavy but inaccurate machine gun fire from an

Armoured Fighting Vehicle (AFV) stationed about 200 yards south of the Kafr Badda Bridge, and from a machine gun post situated under the bridge it self.[7] Using whatever available cover they could find the Section advanced cautiously towards the AFV until they were within 300 yards of the target. Then from a firing position LCpl Bob Tait, armed his Boys anti-tank rifle, and fired three well-aimed shots at the armoured vehicle, scoring a direct hit which set it on fire. The accuracy of Tait's firing and the intentions of the commandos clearly unnerved the enemy manning the machine gun post under the bridge, for shortly after the AFV was hit, the gun under the bridge ceased firing, and the Section crossed safely over the coastal road.

No. 7 Troop, commanded by Lt Paddy Mayne, landed as the centre group of Y Party; the Troop was also accompanied in their landing craft by Sgt Jack Terry's sub-section from No. 1 Troop. The troop came under fire immediately and soon started to take casualties, with one man killed on the beach.[8] Initially they advanced north along the beach for about 400 yards before they turned east and headed inland, by this stage they were also accompanied for a short period by B Section of No.8 Troop, under command of Lt Bill Fraser, which had landed to the left of Mayne's Troop. Fraser's section lost contact with the rest of No.8 Troop and would spent the next hour or so of the operation fighting alongside Mayne's men.

Bill Fraser

Photo courtesy of
National War Museum Scotland

Despite coming under sustained fire from two machine gun posts, No.7 Troop reached the coastal road by 0520hrs. As they took up positions around the objective Mayne spotted a group of soldiers firing in a northerly direction, unsure if they were the enemy or advancing Australians, Mayne crawled forward about 50 yards, through what he described as a hayfield, using the long crop as cover until he was able to hear the men speaking French. Having obtained confirmation that they were in fact enemy troops, Mayne initiated an assault on their position, throwing hand grenades as his men opened up on the startled French Colonial troops.[9] Shocked by Mayne's trademark power and aggression the French very quickly surrendered their position, resulting in the capture of around 40 prisoners, two machine guns and a mortar. With only a couple of his own men hurt, one of which was Lt Robin McCunn who had been injured in the shoulder while leading the Troop's forward sections. Mayne sent McCunn, along with Pte Paxton, back towards the Australian's lines.[10] Having taken the objective Mayne dispatched a runner to inform Dick Pedder of his Troop's success; however, the runner returned having been unable to find the Commanding Officer.[11] Undeterred, Mayne continued with his secondary objective, which was to support X Party, which he has assumed had landed on the north side of the river and not the south. Oblivious to X Party's predicament, Mayne pressed on towards the hills to the north of the barracks, meeting pockets of enemy troops, which offered little resistance. The Troop captured several more prisoners as they went, before Mayne decided to head south-east towards Qasmiye.[12] At about 0630hrs Mayne and his Troop turned south towards the Litani River to support Keyes's X Party. Meanwhile, Bill Fraser and his B Section of No.8 Troop, who had joined forces with Mayne shortly after losing contact with their own

Troop soon after landing on the beach, continued east into the hills, reaching the crest without meeting any opposition. However they soon met resistance from a unit of French Cavalry who had dismounted and taken up positions among the trees. After fire was exchanged several enemy were killed and about 30 prisoners were taken. At this point Fraser's Section met and was joined by a Sub-Section of No.4 Troop, who had landed as part of Capt More's Z Party further up the coast. Having dealt with the French Cavalry, Fraser headed south along the hills without meeting anymore resistance. On reaching the crest of the hill that overlooked the Litani River they were engaged by fire coming from the Australians on the south side of the river. As the Section took up defensive positions on the crest they also came under fire from Australian artillery that were bombarding the ridge, so Fraser soon withdrew his men into cover behind the hill.[13]

Meanwhile Paddy Mayne and No.7 Troop, who had been marching south for about an hour, came across an explosive store from where they captured another 30 prisoners.[14] Determined to push on, Mayne, his men and his prisoners reached the northern bank of the Litani River by about 0800hrs where, like Fraser's Section, they were met by fire from the Australians on the south side of the river. Despite waving a white flag, the agreed sign of friendly forces, they were pinned to the ground for some time. At about 0900hrs they were able to move under cover and concentrated their prisoners at the explosive store.[15] After spending a considerable length of time in the explosives store Mayne decided that he had to keep moving and ordered the Troop to head east into the high ground. Leading the forward section he soon found a track which led them to some tethered mules at what he suspected to be another enemy position. Leading from the front, with his revolver in hand, Mayne surprised a group of about 30 French colonial soldiers, many of which were mule drivers. Calling for them to surrender, one instinctively raised his rifle and Mayne shot him instantly.[16] As Mayne's men searched the position they found typewriters, ammunition, bombs and much to the delight of the commandos, beer and food. As the hungry men were replenishing themselves after about six hours of action, they were disturbed by the ringing of an enemy telephone within the position. Leaving it unanswered they followed the wire which led them to another position where they captured another forty prisoners, four machine guns, two light machine guns and two mortars.[17] Determined to get his Troop back to the Australian lines, Mayne once again headed east before changing direction south towards the Litani River. At about 1700hrs and after a long detour, they arrived back at the river, but once again came under fire from the Australians, who were still on the south side in that area, resulting in one man being killed by friendly fire. Just before dark they were able to cross the Litani by a pontoon bridge that had been erected by Australian sappers from 2/6 Field Company[18], near to the position where the Qasmiye Bridge had stood before being blown up. On crossing the pontoon Mayne and his men, accompanied by about seventy prisoners, marched into the Australian lines before continuing on to Tyre the following day.[19]

Earlier in the day Commando HQ and No.1 Troop were still preoccupied with their advance, and having successfully taken the barracks and 75mm Gun positions, they pushed forward to a ridge 800 yards north east of the barracks, and soon came under heavy machine gun and sniper fire. At this stage Dick Pedder considered the situation to be very serious and issued an order for No. 1 Troop to withdraw to a more favourable position offering better cover further north. Having been told by a runner to report to the

Commanding Officer, Gerald Bryan and his men sprinted over the open ground as the enemy were laying down heavy fire, giving testament to the fitness and determination of the commandos. They got to the CO's position without taking any casualties, but their luck was soon to desert them as the enemy closed in from different directions. With little time to lose, Pedder gave Bryan a set of hasty orders and detailed him to assist with nullifying some enemy snipers. Bryan's men had no option but to take up positions in an area which offered limited cover and it was only a matter of time before they started taking casualties. Gerald Bryan recalls the deteriorating situation for the Party:

We had to cross about 300 yards of open ground to reach the Colonel so we just ran like hell, and although there were a few bullets flying around, I don't think we had a single casualty. I arrived at Commando HQ and reported to the Colonel. He explained that he was pushing in some men and wanted our section to support them and pick off snipers. We took up what positions we could but there wasn't much cover. I left the Colonel and went over to a Bren-gun post about fifty yards away but it took me a good ten minutes to get there as I had to crawl the whole way. The French had spotted us and were putting down a lot of small arms fire - very accurate. The whole time bullets spat past my head and sounded very close. It was very unpleasant and hard to think correctly. When I reached the Bren posts, they were stuck. Every time they tried to fire, a machine gun opened up and they couldn't spot it. Suddenly the B Section officer said he had spotted it and grabbed a rifle, but as he was taking aim he was shot in the chest and went down, coughing blood. Then the Sergeant was shot in the shoulder, from a different direction, which meant we were being fired on from two-fronts.[20]

B Section officer, 23-years-old Lt Alistair Coode, was killed instantly and Sgt Don Robinson was shot in the shoulder and badly wounded. Pedder, meanwhile, had ordered the Commando HQ to retire to the gulley through which they had advanced and to make every endeavour to make contact with Major Keyes' X Party to the south. As they withdrew through the gulley, RSM Tevendale describes the incident that would have a far reaching effect on the destiny of No.11 (Scottish) Commando:

At about 0945 hours I was about 20 yards to the right of the Commanding Officer as we were running for the gulley when I heard him shout, "Tevendale, Farmiloe, I'm shot." I dashed across to him and found that he had been shot through the back and the chest and had died immediately.[21]

The death of the Commanding Officer was a devastating blow to both RSM Tevendale and the rest of the Commando. However, the RSM was a professional soldier, and knew that with Dick Pedder's death, the commandos and especially the younger officers would be looking to him to take control of the situation. As with most soldiers who experience the death of a comrade Tevendale put his emotions to one side and got on with the job he had to do; the time to grieve would happen after the battle. Before leaving the body of his Commanding Officer, Tevendale searched him for important papers but found none, and with Capt Farmiloe assuming command, they moved to the right under cover of some bushes. Accompanied by three riflemen who had joined them from No.1 Troop, Tevendale was ordered by Farmiloe to engage the enemy that had fired on them from the ridge near the barracks.[22]

Robin Farmiloe

Photo courtesy of
National War Museum Scotland

As Tevendale headed for the ridge, Bryan and his section were under intense fire from the enemy, and unaware that Pedder had been killed, Bryan had tried to make contact with the Commanding Officer by crawling under fire back to the Commando HQ; an action that would affect the young officer for the rest of his life:

I crawled back to Commando HQ but when I was about ten yards away, I heard someone shout, "The Colonel's hit. Get the medical orderly." I shouted to the Adjutant Robin Farmiloe and he replied that the Colonel was dead and that he was going to withdraw the attack and try his luck elsewhere. So I shouted to my men to make for some scrub about a hundred yards away and started crawling towards it. All the time bullets were fizzing past much too close for comfort and we kept very low. Sgt Worrall, who had already been wounded, decided to run for it, to catch us up, but a machine gun got him and he fell with his face covered with blood.[23]

During training the commandos were taught to keep the inside of their feet flat on the ground so as to keep their profile as low to the ground as possible.[24] However crawling using that method can be a slow process. In an attempt to cover the ground and reach the scrub quickly, Bryan was crawling with his heels in the air:

I suddenly felt a tremendous bang on the head and I knew I had been hit. However, when I opened my eyes I saw that it was in the legs and decided not to die. I dragged myself into a bit of a dip and tried to get fairly comfortable, but every time I moved, they opened up on us. I could hear an NCO yelling to me to keep down or I would be killed. I kept down.[25]

Litani River

He later described the extent of his injuries and the horrendous conditions he had to endure:

> After a time when the initial shock had worn off the pain in my legs became unbearable I managed to extract and swallow the morphia pill that we carried for such emergencies. There was a gaping wound in my right leg just above the foot and it is bleeding, but I can do nothing about it. My left leg has gone rigid. By now the sun is well up and it is very hot lying there with no cover. I am very thirsty but cannot get a drink. My water bottle is strapped on to my belt on my left side. To get at it I have to raise my elbow above the level of my cover. Each time I to get my water bottle I get a fuselage of fire, so I put up with the thirst and lie hoping that I lose consciousness. After a short time my thirst is so great that I try again. But again I am subject to several rounds of small arms fire. This is repeated several times and I never succeed in getting a drink.[26]

The unfolding situation was looking dire for Y Party, and just as RSM Tevendale had succeeded in clearing the ridge the situation deteriorated further when he was informed by a runner that Capt Farmiloe had been wounded and that none of his party could reach him. Tevendale recalled:

> I immediately returned with the runner and dashed across about 50 yards of open ground under heavy machine gun fire to where Captain Farmiloe was lying. He had sustained a very severe wound to the right temple and had died almost immediately. With great difficulty I reached my party and was informed by one of the party of seven men who had joined HQ from No.1 Troop, that they were all that was left of that Troop, the remainder had either been killed or wounded and taken prisoner.[27]

One of the No.1 Troop prisoners was the wounded Gerald Bryan, who recalled the last moments before being captured by the advancing enemy:

After what seems to be a very long time but was probably about an hour or so there is another fuselage of fire and the next thing I see were about twenty five French soldiers advancing with fixed bayonets. The four men left uninjured in my section stood up with their hands up and are captured. They are all volunteers from Newfoundland. I raise my arm and a French soldier approaches me cautiously. He is carrying a rifle which he cocks ready to fire. He points the rifle at my head from about six inches away and I think, Good God I have survived my wounds only to be butchered in cold blood. I have a French automatic pistol which was given to me by Sgt Worrall in exchange for my rifle. It had actually jammed on the first shot but I had held on to it and I suppose the French soldier felt that he was at risk. I plead for my life but in the crisis I think I am using English only and probably all I am saying in French is, "Thank you." He goes away without doing or saying anything.[28]

About 30 minutes later the four Newfoundlanders return with stretchers under a French NCO guard. The men search the area and retrieve the bodies of Colonel Pedder, Captain Farmiloe and Lt Coode. They also collect the wounded Gerald Bryan and took him to a dressing station where a British medical orderly gave him a shot of morphine. At the dressing station Bryan was reunited, much to his relief, with Sgts Don Robinson and Gordon Worrall, both of whom he thought had been killed on the battlefield. Some time later the trio were taken by ambulance to a casualty clearing station in Sidon, before being transferred to the French Military Hospital in Beirut. On reaching the hospital the extent of Bryan's injuries were soon realised and the French surgeon was left with no option but to amputate his right leg below the knee with a guillotine.[29]

With the deaths of both Pedder and Farmiloe, RSM Tevendale assumed command of the depleted Y Party, and his first decision was to try and make contact with Keyes, but this proved impractical and he soon decided against it. After reassessing the situation Tevendale decided to advance through the barracks area, splitting his men into small rifle parties and by using the available cover, they soon made it safely to a ridge about 300 yards to the South of the barracks facing the direction of the Litani River. The ridge commanded the main road that ran to the barracks and was the main line of communication to the enemy's forward positions. The party had previously cut this line of communication to the enemy's HQ and from the ridge they were able to prevent enemy runners from getting back to the HQ which was about 500 yards behind to the right of their position on the ridge.

At about 1300 hours the Australian Artillery laid down a heavy barrage of fire around the party's position, causing the enemy to retire to a position to the rear of Tevendale's party. As the enemy made their way to the position in the rear, the party was able to pick them off and inflicted heavy casualties on them. However Tevendale and the remainder of the party were unable to sustain the attack and by about 1700 hours they were surrounded and captured.

CHAPTER 9
LITANI RIVER – Z PARTY

9/10 June 1941

Z Party commanded by Capt George More, was made up of No.10 Troop under the command of Lt Tommy Macpherson and No.4 Troop led by Lt Eion McGonigal; for administration purposes Commando Troops were paired together to form Squadrons, Capt Ian McDonald was Squadron Commander for No's 4 and 10 Troop and operated under Captain More.[1] Z Party's intention was to prevent supplies reaching the enemy position and to reinforce Y Party if possible.[2] More further detailed that No.10 Troop was to seize the Kafr Badda Bridge and that No.4 Troop were to support them if necessary otherwise it was to manoeuvre and support Y Party; Z Party HQ were to accompany McGonigal's No.4 Troop.[3]

By around 0420hrs Z Party's ALC's, Nos 2, 4 and 6, had all reached Beach D.[4] ALC No.6 made a good landing, with the commandos only having to wade for about ten yards in two feet of water before reaching the beach.[5] However ALC No.2 struck a reef and had to disembark into about seven feet of water.[6] Tommy Macpherson recalls the landing:

Our objective was to clear a bridge called Kafr Badda crossing the rocky wadi on the main north/south highway. Sitting in the landing craft with its high sides the passengers cannot of course see out. We grounded on a sandbar and in accordance with standard drills exited at the double, only for the first chaps to disappear completely below the waves, since we had hit a sandbar that was some ten yards offshore and deep water intervened. The immediate preoccupation therefore was to form a human chain that got people and their weapons ashore, with the Navy reversing rapidly away, we realised we were on the south or wrong side of the wadi.[7]

As with Geoffrey Keyes's X Party, elements of Z Party had been landed at the wrong location and on the wrong side of the enemy. The intention had been for No.10 Troop to land north of the wadi and therefore attack the enemy positions around the bridge from the rear. Landing to the south and in clear view of the enemy they soon came under fire. Pte Frank Varney, a former colliery banksman, who had enlisted with the Sherwood Foresters, recalled a lucky escape for his friend Pte George Dove:

A bullet cut through the strap of George Dove's steel helmet, went right on through the top of it, and then ricocheted into his seat. He had always talked of showing his scars, and here was one he couldn't show to anybody![8]

Despite being shot in the backside, Dove continued to fight on and carried his Bren gun for the remainder of the operation, however not all were so fortunate, as Jimmy Lappin recalled:

We had just cleared the beach and were lying in scrub grass. It was just after dawn on a beautiful clear morning. The air was still and when I looked over to the next two blokes, McKay and Hurst, a couple of yards away, they had just lit up cigarettes. I could see two thin columns of blue smoke rising and I thought that I would have a smoke too but, just as I got my cigarettes out, the whistle blew for us to advance. These two blokes never moved, they were both hit, the smoke gave away their position.[9]

Cpl. Robert McKay, Queens Own Cameron Highlanders was killed outright and Pte Ben Hurst, King's Own Royal Regiment (Lancaster) died later in the day.

McGonigals No.4 Troop fared no better, Bren-gunner Cpl H. Butler recalled the wet start to the operation:

We waded ashore in a heavy sea, over rocks, and each wave breaking over our heads and shoulders. We covered the last 40 yards to shore under machine-gun fire and advanced 150 yards inland without casualties, took cover and discarded lifebelts and haversacks as previously planned. Then we advanced in open formation due east...I spotted a machine-gun nest at our rear and took aim. The Bren refused to fire, so I made for cover and stripped it down, found it full of water and sand. Laid low for almost half an hour cleaning it. When clean I reassembled it and found the French MG post had moved.[10]

Fellow No.4 Troop member Reg Harmer remembers the confusion of the first attempted landing on 8 June and the events of actual landing on 9 June:

We were going to do the landing in three lots you see, we were going to go and land about half past one in the morning, we got down in the ALCs and we were manoeuvring round to form up formation to go into the beach...the commander of the operation he called us all back to the boat, we all got back on our boat, we had the Glengyle, we left there and went into Port Said, never bloody stopped, washing went up on the Naval tower, we never stopped went straight back...to the same spot, identical spot, and they were waiting weren't they, they couldn't believe their luck, and of course it was broad daylight...and of course we got there on the beach and of course they opened up firing on us and we opened up firing on them and we all rushed around in our ALCs and got formed up and off we go onto the beach, there was a reef there long before you get onto the beach, so the ALCs went up in the air, down went the front, cos they couldn't go and where we had to jump off, it was ten foot of bloody water, so we had to swim until we could get our feet on the bottom.[11]

The wet start to operation brought with it its own problems for Z Party's commander, George More's only means of communicating with the other Commando Parties, a No.18 Wireless Set, and with the Australians, a No.11 Set, had both been damaged during the landing and therefore no form of wireless communication was available to him, a set back that he detailed in his report:

> 0420 - A.L.Cs landed in correct position, but my A.L.C. hit a rock some 80 yards from the shore. All men landed safely, but both wirelesses were rendered useless.[12]

By 0430hrs McGonigal's No.4 Troop, with 2nd Lt Geoffrey Parnacott and three Sub-Sections had cleared the beach without any casualties, and headed due east over the main coastal road towards the high ground to east of the Kafa Badda Bridge. At about 0440hrs Capt More's party and 2nd Lt Charles Richards's Section crossed the coastal road and observed four enemy trucks stop in the low ground ahead of them (Point A on More's Sketch Map), and unload two Hotchkiss heavy machine guns with the intention of firing them at Dick Pedder's Y Party.[13] More and Richard's Section took up a position on a spur and engaged the enemy, killing and wounding several of them before the remainder surrendered. In the meantime Lt Parnacott's Section had taken cover in some trees bordering the coastal road, and from the cover Sgt Charlie Hill spotted a shallow ravine which entered into a low range of hills. In arrowhead formation the Section crossed the road and proceeded up the ravine without incurring any fire, but as the ravine came to an abrupt end against a low hill, the Section was halted while Sgt Hill followed by Lt Parnacott climbed to the top and viewed the ground ahead of them. Observing a large house about 150 yards to their front Parnacott instructed Hill to take two men and clear the house.[14] Accompanied by Cpl Severn and one other, Hill led the party to the house where, using a combination of grenades and machine gun fire, cleared the house killing two occupants, one an enemy soldier and the other an unfortunate civilian who was caught in the blast from the grenades.[15]

Charles Hill

Photo courtesy of
Hill Collection

With the house clear Parnacott's Section continued with the advance towards the summit of the hill where they were greeted by a hail of mortar shells and machine gun fire. As the commandos took cover Parnacott called up Reg Harmer and his anti tank rifle who effectively dealt with the enemy positions which were situated about 300 yards away on the north side of the valley to the north east of the Kafr Badda Bridge. As the enemy deserted their positions they were picked off with some excellent marksmanship from the Section's riflemen and from Cpl Butler, the Section's Bren gunner, all from a range of about 300 yards. The fighting, however, was not all one way, and four of Parnacott's men were wounded in the exchanges. The wounded were taken back over the hill where LCpl Jackson, one of the Commando's medical orderlies was ready to treat them as best he could. Among the four was LCpl Fred Fleke whose lower jaw and shoulder were badly injured.[16]

Meanwhile the remainder of McGonigal's No.4 Troop, which had already crossed the coastal road, had reached the high ground to the east of the bridge (Point C on More's Sketch Map) and were able to observe More and Richards's section engaging the enemy; from their position they gave covering fire for as long as possible and once they saw that the enemy had surrendered they pushed northwards along the hills towards the Kafr Badda Bridge.[17] About 40 prisoners were rounded up before George More sent Richards and his Section south to support Pedder's Y Party. More then organised guards for the prisoners and a temporary Regimental Aid Post (RAP) for the wounded. Landing in the same ALC as More, Piper Jimmy Lawson, who was one of the Party's medical orderlies, quickly helped to set up the RAP and was soon dealing with a number of casualties.

It was around this time that George More came across Sgt Jack Terry and his Sub-Section from No.1

Troop who had strayed away from Y Party during the landing further down the beach. More instructed Terry to stay with Z Party to support the attack on the bridge. In the meantime, at about 0500hrs, as No.4 Troop advanced northwards, an enemy armoured truck and armoured car were observed on the road running east from the Kafr Badda Bridge; the Troop engaged the enemy destroying the truck but the armoured car managed to escape to the east. From their position they also observed around twenty enemy soldiers retiring to the north towards the bridge; with the advantage of the high ground, they engaged them with small arms fire from about 300 yards with good effect.[18] A short while later, at around 0630hrs, after enemy activity had been detected to the east of the Kafr Badda Bridge (Point D on More's Sketch Map), More, Parnacott's Section and Sgt Jack Terry's Sub-Section advanced to the east along the valley where they found four enemy 155mm howitzers.[19] After instructing the remainder of his section to give covering fire Parnacott accompanied by Sgt Hill, Cpl Severn and Pte Taylor closed in on the position, only to find, much to their surprise a dishevelled and demoralised group of soldiers, many of whom were lying face down or lying close to the walls of the cover. Parnacott and Hill were soon joined by the rest of the Section who immediately started to round up and disarm the prisoners. In the meantime Hill and some men, less Pte Taylor who had been wounded in the thigh, went to investigate a number of enemy trucks which were situated about 400 yards further along the valley. As they approached two French Officers walked out of a field kitchen with their hands in the air and were duly captured; a search of the area resulted in no more enemy being found.[20]

Meanwhile, A Section of No.8 Troop commanded by Capt Ian Glennie, who earlier had destroyed an enemy AFV with Bob Taits anti-tank rifle south of the Kafr Badda Bridge before proceeding east towards the hills, met Lt McGonigal who informed Glennie about the battery of enemy guns and the large quantity of enemy transport that was situated in the Kafr Badda valley (Point D). Glennie immediately decided to launch an attack on the enemy position from the east to correspond with the assault that was being mounted by Parnacott's troops from the west.[21] Glennie's attack which started around 0630hrs was met with some resistance resulting in a few casualties taken by the Party; however the artillerymen were no match for the dogged and determined commandos and in no time at all they put down their arms and surrendered. Among those captured were a number of Senegalese artillerymen and the two French officers who surrendered at the field kitchen. One of them later explained that the battery was unable to fire the Howitzers as the telephone lines to his Observation Post (OP) had been cut.[22]

Earlier in the morning at around 0425hrs, No.10 Troop, having made it ashore, came under small arms fire as they crossed the beach (Point B on More's Sketch Map). With little available cover they pushed on until the fire ceased about five minutes later, enabling them to continue their advance inland towards their objective, which was the Kafr Badda Bridge on the main coast road.[23] Fifteen minutes later at 0445hrs, as No.4 Troop were engaging the enemy to the east of the Kafr Badda Bridge, No.10 Troop were advancing across flat open ground when they came under very heavy small arms and canon fire from an enemy strong point, which included armoured cars, just to the east of the bridge. With one machine gun position on the enemy left and three machine gun positions on the rising ground on the enemy right [24] (Point F on More's Sketch Map), No.1 and No.4 Sub-Sections were pinned to the ground under the heavy fire. However No.2 Sub-Section and Troop HQ managed to get round to the right flank while No.3 Sub-Section got round to the left. During the course of the attack on the enemy position one armoured car was set on fire and the crew killed, while the remaining vehicles were either burnt or put out of action. Tommy Macpherson recalls the attack:

> We were clearly expected because as soon as we left the narrow bridge, which was protected by an upward slope and merged on the flat plain, machine guns opened from the Kafr Badda position. There was very little option but to make a frontal assault with such covering fire as we could give from our Bren guns. The distance was about three quarters of a mile. I am bound to say it seemed much longer at the time and as rehearsed, we advanced in a widely spread order of individual diagonal rushes. Fortunately the opposition had dug in with a strength of one platoon plus some mortar support and two medium machine guns in a fairly small ring around the bridge and consisted of Lebanese French troops of somewhat unenthusiastic quality. They did not wait for our final assault but left a rear party, poor chaps, and beetled off under cover of rocks and bushes to another prepared position about 300 yards further back. We over ran the bridge and then of course it was necessary to assault the prepared position which otherwise would have made life uncomfortable. That did not prove too difficult as they had been expecting an attack from the east or up the road and had left their northern flank exposed which was on rising ground and overlooked the position itself. The opposition therefore was forced to evacuate that position and disappear in transport, leaving behind a number of casualties and all their heavier weapons.[25]

As Macpherson went into the position to take the surrender he was attacked by an enemy soldier who stuck his bayonet into the young officer's wrist, an action that cost the Senegalese infantryman his life; no sooner had he made the attack than he was promptly shot by Sgt Charlie Bruce.[26] While No.10 Troop was securing the area around the bridge, an ambulance appeared from the north side. Giving the enemy a chance to evacuate their dead and wounded, the commandos were ordered to hold their fire. However, they watched in amazement as the ambulance crew unloaded a heavy mortar, an action that proved futile because by that stage the commandos were much too close for the mortar to be of any use.[27]

By around 0800hrs Z Party had begun to consolidate the position around the Kafr Badda Bridge. Capt. More had assembled all his party: No.4 Troop less Lt Richards's A Section, No.10 Troop and Sgt Terry's sub-section of No.1 Troop, in the vicinity of the high ground to the south east of the bridge (Point C). Then in accordance with his original orders he placed his troops in defensive positions around the bridge, No.10 Troop was positioned on the high ground to the north-east of the bridge [28] (Point F on More's Sketch Map) and No.4 Troop on the hills overlooking the valley some 500 yards east of No.10 Troop.[29] More then decided to assemble all the prisoners taken so far in a central camp (Point D on More's Sketch Map) east of the Kafr Badda Bridge in the valley where the trucks and field kitchen were located and two French officers had been captured. Responsibility for guarding the camp was left to McGonigal's No.4 Troop and Sgt Terry's Sub-Section. Within an hour the prisoners were all under guard and the wounded were taken care of; an RAP and temporary HQ was established and the Party was fed on French tinned meat and pork from the field kitchen.[30]

At around 0800hrs, with Macpherson and his men in their defensive positions, enemy reconnaissance aircraft were spotted flying over the position being held by Z Party. Approximately ninety minutes later, at 0930hrs, three enemy AFVs were observed by the forward troops, advancing cautiously south towards the bridge along the main coastal road. From the vantage point of the high ground the commandos were able to engage the AFVs as soon as they were in range, and with no desire to put up a fight, the AFVs withdrew immediately, with the rear vehicle giving covering fire in the process.[31] Around this time two French destroyers, Guerpard and Valmy [32] appeared from the north. Macpherson recalls the incident:

The sun proceeded to shine and quite an agreeable day developed. The noteworthy incident was the appearance offshore, coming from the north, of two hostile destroyers who proceeded to fire quite a number of rounds from their main armament in our general direction. It was really quite fascinating watching through binoculars the gun turrets swing round until you felt you were practically looking down the barrels, but either their shooting was inaccurate or they had no clear idea where our position was, since the nearest rounds fell a good 200 yards away.[33]

As the destroyers carried on down the coast the Australians on the south side of the Litani River were not as fortunate as Macpherson and his commandos; at around 1030 hrs the 2/16 Battalion HQ and artillery areas were shelled suffering a direct hit causing two deaths.[34] For Z Party there then followed a lull of about ninety minutes, during which an investigation was carried out by No.10 Troop to ensure that the bridge was not mined. The Troop were also detailed to carry out a search of the various captured vehicles, during which maps and papers were found which were to prove useful to the Australians later on in the operation. The lull however was short lived; at around 1140hrs the enemy returned along the same road in five armoured cars launching attacks from various distances from the Troop's position. Firstly they open up with machine gun and cannon fire from 1500–2000 yards, searching the position inaccurately at first, but becoming more accurate later as they started to identify the Troop's location. The armoured cars then advanced forward, probing the ground while giving fire and manoeuvre cover to each other until they were within 450 yards of the commando's position. With the enemy now in range the commandos were ordered to open fire, an action that caused them to quickly retire back along the road.[35] As the day progressed the destroyers and armoured cars were not the only source of annoyance for the Troop, and during the afternoon the enemy deployed several machine gun and canon positions in broken ground out of range of the Troop. These positions had a very clear view and caused them a lot of bother.[36]

Meanwhile, 2nd Lt Charles Richards and his Section, who had earlier been sent by More to support Y Party, had met Lt Bill Fraser's Section accompanied by a Sub-Section from No.4 Troop. Fraser and his men had been taking cover behind the hill after earlier being fired on by the Australians on the south side as they had approached the river from the north. As Richards and Fraser were planning the next move for their Sections it was observed that, from a position on the hills to the right, the enemy was directing heavy fire towards the previously demolished Qasmiye Bridge, which was situated further to the east of the river from where Geoffrey Keyes and his men were trying to cross. With no time to waste the two Sections combined to work as a Troop and attacked the positions from the rear, with Fraser's B

Section, dealing with three machine gun posts on the forward southern slope. The enemy had gathered in some strength in the woods on the ridge of the hill, and in addition to those killed and wounded, many prisoners were taken.[37]

Before the successful attack Fraser and Richards had agreed that after the positions on the hill had been taken they would turn north and advance towards the area where More and Z Party were, as they had both been puzzled by the lack of their own troops in that area. Meeting little opposition they made contact with More about 1730hrs, and took up a defensive position to the right of the Z Party position around the Kafr Badda Bridge. During this phase in the operation Fraser had handed over command of the section to Sgt Cheyne, as he had suffered concussion from a wound to the head.[38]

Meanwhile earlier in the day, George More had previously instructed Sgt Hill and Driver Foster to take two of the captured enemy Hotchkiss heavy machine guns and 50,000 rounds of ammunition to No.10 Troop's position at the Kafr Badda Bridge. He left on a motorcycle that he had found among the captured enemy vehicles, to gather up prisoners and the wounded from a holding point, that had been set up south of the Kafr Badda Bridge on the main costal road (Point A), and move them to the new camp that was being guarded by members of No.4 Troop and Jack Terry's men in the valley to the east of the bridge (Point D). At around 0800hrs More then headed south on the motorcycle and about 30mins later, while trying to make contact with the Commando's right, he found that Aiteniye was being heavily shelled. As he rounded a corner he was fired upon by an Australian heavy machine gun coming from the south of the Litani River. Despite carrying a large white towel to use as a white flag, the agreed recognition symbol, his motor cycle was shot from underneath him and he only managed to escape with great difficulty.[39]

While More was heading south by motorcycle, and during a lull in the shelling, Lt Parnacott decided to try and move some of the wounded men back to the Commando HQ. Accompanied by Sgt Hill they loaded ten wounded men into the back of a commandeered truck and with Parnacott driving they headed south along the coast road. With a white handkerchief attached to the top of the truck they were no more than five minutes into their journey when the shelling resumed accompanied by small arms fire. With no option but to abort the journey, Parnacott skilfully turned the truck around. However with the fire intensifying both he and Hill were left with no option but to dive from the cab of the truck and take cover from the incoming fire in the roadside ditch. As the rounds rattled into the truck they soon realised that the wounded men were in grave danger and simultaneously they leapt from the ditch and within seconds were back in the truck and heading a great speed back along the road towards Kafr Badda closely followed by enemy fire. Once they were well out of the range of the enemy fire they stopped the vehicle and checked on the fate of the wounded men in the rear. With the trucks canvas cover riddled with bullet holes it was of no great surprise that they found that two of the wounded had been killed by the incoming fire.[40]

In the meantime Capt Glennie and No.8 Troop's A Section had also found themselves a mechanised mode of transport. After handing over their prisoners to McGonigal at Point D, A Section boarded a captured enemy truck and headed south along the coast road with the intention of reinforcing the troops from Y Party, who were attacking the barracks on the high ground to the east.[41] After travelling about 800 yards they came across Capt More who was returning from his skirmish with the enemy, and he informed

Glennie about his encounter and of the position of a machine gun post that was further down the road. Glennie debussed the men from the truck and set off on foot in a south easterly direction with the intention of finding and destroying the machine gun post.[42]

More meanwhile returned to inspect the defensive positions and the camp at Point D, before leaving at around 1000hrs with Sgt Hill to try again to establish contact with the Commando HQ to the south. More and Hill decided to avoid the costal road and instead travelled via the hills.[43] However by 1100hrs they came under heavy and close range machine gun fire near the barracks and withdrew with great difficulty.

Earlier Glennie's forward Sub-Section had came under heavy and accurate machine gun fire from the north-east and east of the barracks and before long was soon pinned to the ground. The reserve Sub-Section, however, made its way down a valley with the intention of taking the position from the rear. As they were moving they encountered the withdrawing Capt More and Sgt Hill who informed them that they had also been fired on by the machine gun post from the same positions at the barracks.[44]

At around 1200hrs, and having earlier been reinforced by two men with a light machine gun from No.4 Troop, More and Glennie decided to form a scratch Section with the intention of locating and silencing the offending machine gun. With More leading the forward Sub-Section the make-shift party set off again to try and locate the machine gun position. After a short while the forward Sub-Section was fired on by a further hidden machine gun position and as a result suffered one casualty; meanwhile Glennie's reserve Sub-Section had moved around to the right but was also fired on and pinned to the ground by a machine gun post that they were unable to locate. Glennie's Sub-Section was now in an untenable position and had no other option but to retire back to the coast road, where it tried unsuccessfully to make contact with More and his men.[45]

As Glennie's Sub-Section was reorganising on the coast road, heavy fire broke out further along the road in the direction of the Kafr Badda Bridge, where several AFVs were observed approaching the position. At that point Glennie decided to drop back and reinforce No.10 Troop, knowing that the two Boys' anti-tank rifles that he had in his party would be best served over by the bridge. However as they approached the reserve position of No.10 Troop, they encountered heavy and accurate fire and suffered a number of casualties. Nevertheless the sub-section soon took up a position to the left of No.10 Troop.

The attacks on No. 10 Troop at the Kafr Badda Bridge had continued steadily throughout the day, and by 1730hrs the enemy had eight armoured cars and some mortars in the area of the coast road. During the afternoon the Troop had managed to damage one armoured car and put the guns of another out of action, but the eight armoured cars were soon to be joined by another six which took up positions on the right flank, the area which was being held by a detachment of No. 6 Troop. However the detachment withdrew without warning and left the flank uncovered.[46] The enemy then attacked the forward defensive positions from both flanks with armoured cars and infantry. At about 1730hrs a runner who had been sent by Capt McDonald, to find Capt More, and give a picture of the position, returned with a message to disengage and withdraw.[47] The Troop was forced to withdraw to the next ridge at about 1800hrs as the advancing enemy released and rearmed a large number of prisoners and started to out flank the commandos.

Meanwhile, No.4 Troop who had spent most of the day positioned some 500 yards to the east of No.10

Troop, on the hills overlooking the valley. In his report Eion McGonigal later detailed the situation on the ground:

We held this position till about four o'clock in the afternoon, and during this time we set up a very temporary R.A.P. and had under our care a large body of prisoners. During this period we saw small bodies of the enemy to the eastward, all of these retiring northwards, and a French reconnaissance plane made repeated flights over us in the early afternoon. We could hear the sounds of No.10 Troop on our left engaging the enemy A.F.V.s on the main north road, and at four o'clock six armoured cars appeared on the road running to our east about 1400 yards away. These A.F.V.s engaged our area with two pounders or some similar gun, and medium M.G.s. They inflicted heavy casualties on our French prisoners. It had been impossible owing to the flat nature of the ground around the road, to put anti-A.F.V. obstacles on the road and so on the approach of the A.F.V.s I withdrew my main body consisting of one sub-section of No.4 Troop and some dozen men from Nos.1,7 and 10 Troops, whom I had formed into another sub-section. One sub-section and two A/Tk rifles stayed in our area and were driven out by A.F.V.s some fifteen minutes later. We reformed in the hills and with three sub-sections and two A/Tk rifles we moved to the support of No.10 Troop. During the action with the A.F.V's many French prisoners were killed attempting to disarm our men or to escape.[48]

With the situation becoming increasingly ominous for Z Party, McGonigal's No.4 Troop had moved to support No.10 Troop, and a Sub-Section was sent to a position about 500 yards south of No.10 Troop, to hold the main ridge covering the coastal road.[49] Then McGonigal, with the remainder of the Troop, reported to Capt McDonald and placed himself under his orders. As McGonigal's No.4 Troop took up their defensive positions they were accompanied by Capt Glennie's A Section, who had also moved over to reinforce No.10 Troop. Capt More, who had returned from the attack on the machine gun positions near the barracks, then took command of the Party and having assessed the situation ordered a withdrawal south towards the Litani River using the ridges as bounds, with No.10 Troop and No.4 Troop alternating as the forward troops.[50] As No.10 Troop started to withdraw, Glennie and his party, who were positioned to the left of No.10 Troop, also began to withdraw. Using a succession of ridges that ran at right angles to the coastal road they withdrew south, maintaining a distance of between 300 and 500 yards from the road in order to be able to keep it covered with anti-tank rifle fire.[51] This tactic proved useful for, shortly after they started to withdraw, six armoured cars appeared from the north, with two travelling cross country and four manoeuvring down the coastal road. Glennie's men responded with LMG and anti-tank rifle fire, scoring several hits on the advancing AFVs. For ten minutes the enemy subjected the commandos to heavy fire from close range before retiring from where they came. During the exchanges the Glennie's Section had suffered no casualties.[52]

With the enemy bringing heavy but inaccurate fire on the withdrawing troops, More held a conference with Glennie, McGonigal and Parnacott at 1800hrs. An assessment of the situation did nothing to quell their fears, a head count showed that they were down to about twenty four officers and men,[53] contact with No.10 Troop had been lost, and with the enemy dominating the high ground and the barracks behind them and advancing in great numbers from the front, the party felt as if they were completely cut off.[54] With the situation deteriorating rapidly More decided that the only option was to wait for night to fall before heading west to the coastal road and then south past Aiteniye from where they would head for the Litani River, where it would be their intention to swim across to the safety of Australian lines. They held their position until about 2100hrs before More moved out of the cover to try and find No.10 Troop. Unable to find the isolated Troop, More returned to the Party and at around 2130hrs gave the order for them begin their withdrawal towards the beach. By 2200hrs More, Glennie, McGonigal, Parnacott, and the group of men from A Section No.8 Troop, No.4 Troop and remnants of various other troops, had reached the beach and hid undercover until the moon had advanced and the artillery activity subsided.[55] They sat tight until about 0030hrs before they moved south along the beach. No opposition was met until they reached Aiteniye, where, while in the process of cutting through a double apron wire fence, they were opened up on by a two machine guns and a cannon from a range of about 40 yards.[56] The group suffered several casualties including Lt Parnacott, Sgt Chisolm, Sgt Smith and two other ranks killed and three wounded.[57] As Chisolm and Smith were cut down in the first hail of bullets, Parnacott threw himself to the ground for cover, at the same time removing the pin out of a hand grenade. Shouting for everyone to take cover, Parnacott bravely raised his body from the cover to throw the grenade and was hit squarely in the head by the machine gun fire. Parnacott died instantly still holding the grenade in his hand, in another act of unselfish bravery Sgt Crockett who was close by successfully reached him and relieved him of the grenade.[58] Unable to move forward or backwards the commandos eventually surrendered to the French. Later in his report Ian Glennie describes the action in the last few hours of the operation:

No opposition was met till Aiteniye was reached. Here fire was opened at a range of 40 yds by 2 M.G. and 1 cannon just as Sgt McCubbin, Capt. More, Lt Parnacott and Lt McGonigal and myself had succeeded in cutting through a double apron wire fence. Fire was also opened up on this party by a M.G. post about 100 yds inland, and by L.M.G.s from positions on the bank of the River Litani. This last position was at the time held by our own troops, that is, about 0200hrs on the 10th June. The situation was impossible, 4 men had been killed and 2 wounded and I decided to surrender.[59]

As the rest of the party handed themselves over to the French, one man made a daring escape, L/Cpl Bob Tait, who would later serve with great distinction in the SAS, managed to make his way to the sea and swim along the coast line without being detected until he reached the safety of Geoffrey Keyes position.

George More later reported that while they were held prisoner they were treated well by the French and that the enemy had attended to the wounded commandos. However by 0830hrs on 10 June, having observed the advancing Australian A.F.Vs, the French officer commanding the Aiteniye post surrendered to Capt More. As the Australians took over the positions the remainder of the party rejoined the main body of the Commando under Major Keyes at about 1015hrs.

Meanwhile earlier the previous evening No.10 Troop and the remainder of Z Party had begun to withdraw from the area around the Kafr Badda Bridge. Around 1900hrs, with the enemy advance intensifying, No.10 Troop withdrew a further 250 yards to another position which they held until 1945hrs, by this time the enemy had twenty AFVs on the Troop's left and the infantry was advancing on the high ground to the right with their machine guns still covering the front. The Troop prepared to withdraw as Macpherson later recalled the situation:

> I took three of the four sub-sections back to a defensive position about a mile south by slightly east, which I had already reconnoitred. MacDonald followed with the balance, LCpl Sproule covering. This position was well off both the roads and the armoured cars, after an abortive attempt wherein one was brewed up by the anti-tank rifle, could only give indirect and inaccurate covering fire. The enemy, who were in fair numbers, tried an infantry attack, which was repulsed, leaving about 10 prisoners in our hands. Dusk was now approaching and MacDonald withdrew south east with two subsections to a pinpoint in some wooded ground. It was agreed that I would hold on until dark and then join him in the withdrawal across the Litani. We had to travel together as, owing to the hasty mounting of the operation, there was only one map per troop, which MacDonald had. After dark, we turned the disarmed prisoners loose, having first removed their boots, socks and trousers, and made for our RV. MacDonald was no longer there. He told me later that he thought they had been spotted by patrols and decided to move at once. Fortunately I had studied the map pretty closely, so we made a successful march through the darkness to the river, the other ranks following with an air of unrelieved pessimism and disbelief! [60]

LCpl Sproule had covered the withdrawal to the last possible moment with a captured enemy machine gun that he destroyed before leaving. Macpherson had led his men eastwards following the inland curve which took them up on to a rough plateau intersected by shallow ravines. Shortly afterwards they were alerted by a couple of rifle shots coming from what looked like to him as an almost medieval fortification. Taking advantage of the poorly defended rear of the building they were able to mount an attack fairly easily across the dead ground to the rear. The attack was met without much resistance, and fairly soon almost a Platoon of terrified French Lebanese troops under the command of a sergeant, were in their custody. Taking them with them was not an option, so Macpherson ordered them to remove their trousers, socks and boots, which were dumped along with their weapons some distance away.[61]

Earlier in the evening, Bill Fraser's B Section of No. 8 Troop, which had been in a defensive position to the right of the Kafr Badda Bridge, was also given the order to withdraw. With Fraser still suffering from concussion the Section led by Sgt Cheyne started to move out at around 2000hrs. They withdrew eastwards into the hills without suffering any casualties, before heading south-east in order to try and cross the Litani River on the left of the French positions. As they approached the river at about 0030hrs they met Lt McCunn and Pte Paxton from No.7 Troop. McCunn, who had been wounded in the shoulder earlier in the day, had decided that he and Paxton, who had treated McCunn's wound as best he could, would take cover in the woods before attempting to reach the Australian lines under the cover of darkness. At around 0330hrs, after a few hours rest, Sgt Cheyne and Sgt Nicol swam across the river, and located a suitable crossing place. A line was strung across the river, a chain formed, and the river was successfully forded. The Section including McCunn and Paxton then headed south-westerly towards Tyre, and at about 1130hrs on 10 June they met an Australian artillery battery. Fraser later reported that three men had been left behind to guard the prisoners and contact had been lost, however they managed to cross the river from a point lower down and got back safely.

Macpherson and his party meanwhile had reached the vicinity of the Litani without any further incident, once on the last slope leading down to the river he left the men and went forward with L/Cpl Varney to reconnoitre the river approach; he later recalled:

> Eventually we reached a sharp escarpment which I guessed went down to the river. The troops were getting tired by then, which tends to increase noise, so I decided to leave them on top and go down with L/Cpl Varley to see what the crossing was like and whether there was any risk of it being defended. As we went down we gradually heard the water of the river. I left Varley, who had a Thomson gun, at a point which we judged to be halfway and reasonably commanding and proceeded quietly down until I found myself in the ditch beside the road which clearly ran alongside the river. There luck intervened on our side. I heard a noise and retreated in invisibility. A local white robed Arab came past, complete with donkey and not 50 yards further down the track I heard him halted and challenged by clearly a hostile standing patrol. I therefore returned to Varley and went down to the track and waited. Sure enough, when the circus began, with lots of fireworks, the enemy patrol broke for the east along the road, where we halted them sharply and they obligingly surrendered. Again this consisted of Lebanese soldiers, about ten in number and one French officer. We treated the soldiers as before, leaving them stranded and taking the officer with us, later handing him over to the Australians.[62]

The next task facing Macpherson was to select a suitable crossing point in order to ford the river; he chose a position that was about 20 yards wide, about 5 feet deep and quite fast flowing. Macpherson tested the point himself by crossing it twice, before bringing the men over in single file, each man holding the loose tail of the webbing equipment of the man in front of him. However before Pte Jock Herd, who was a very weak swimmer, attempted to cross he walked a good distance up the river bank before jumping in and getting swept down river where he was caught and pulled ashore by Macpherson and the men on the south bank.[63] With nearly half the party over safely Pte Dunnachie lost his footing and was swept away screaming blue murder. He had been torpedoed in the Athenia at the beginning of the war and had a fear of water.[64] As Dunnachie was being swept away, Macpherson called to Sgt McCulloch to keep the line closed up and moving, before diving after and rescuing him about 20 yards downstream. Dunnachie's shouts had alerted a French post about 500 yards further downstream on the North bank, who responded by firing wildly in the direction of the party.

At that stage L/Cpl Dove, whose injured leg was beginning to stiffen badly, stumbled and fell in the water but was quickly seized and held upright by Cpl Goodgrove. However immediately behind, and encumbered by his anti-tank rifle, L/Cpl 'Hoofy' MacKay, called Hoofy because if his unusually clumsy feet, tripped over Dove's rescuer and was quickly swept downstream in the direction of enemy fire. Macpherson once again came to the rescue, catching up with him quite a long way down the river and with great difficulty he managed to get the much bigger man out of the water. MacKay was by this stage unconscious, but Macpherson promptly administered artificial respiration, and he came spluttering back to life. With the rest of the party safely across the river and on to the south bank, they moved out of the area and headed towards the Australian position on the coast.

CHAPTER 10
LITANI RIVER: NO QUARTER

YParty meanwhile under the command of RSM Tevendale had remained captured by the enemy until they were released by an advancing Australian patrol at about 0330hrs on the morning of 10 June. Tevendale took time to point out to the Officer in Charge of patrol most of the enemy machine gun posts in the area, which by that stage had mostly been vacated. He then commandeered a French motor car, which had been captured the previous day, and evacuated four injured men to the Australian Field Hospital. On the way the car came under heavy machine gun fire from two posts which had been re-manned by the enemy earlier in the morning, but he managed to drive through it and get the men safely to the hospital without incurring any further injuries. Having evacuated the injured men Tevendale reported to the Australian HQ; on his return journey he encountered No.7 Troop led by Paddy Mayne and gave him brief details of what had taken place.[1] Paddy Mayne, who was Mentioned In Dispatches for his part in the operation, left the Commando soon after returning from Syria, although he never wrote an official report on the actions of No.7 Troop during the operation. Mayne, who would go on to command the Special Air Service and become the most decorated soldier in the war, however did write a detailed account of the Troop's exploits in a letter to his brother dated 15 July 1941:

I have left the Scottish Commando now - it was not the same when the CO got written off. Nearly a year I was with it and I liked it well, but I think the Commandos are finished out here. We did a good piece of work when we landed behind the French lines at the Litani River. We were fired on as we landed, but got off the beach with a couple of casualties. Then we saw a lot of men and transport about 600 yards up the road. I couldn't understand it as they seemed to be firing the wrong way, but might have been Aussies. There was quite a lot of cover - kind of hayfield - I crawled up to thirty yards or so and heard them talking French. So I started whaling grenades at them and my men opened fire. After about five minutes, up went a white flag. There were about forty of them - two machine-guns and a mortar - a nice bag to start with. We had only a couple of men hurt. They had been firing at McGonigal's crowd who had landed further north. We left those prisoners and pushed on. McCunn, a Cameronian, was in charge of my forward section and he got stuck, so we went around him. I had about fifteen men. It got hilly and hard going and Frenchies all over the place. Eventually, we came to a path which we followed and came on a dozen mules and one knew that there must be something somewhere and we came on it just around the corner. About thirty of those fellows sitting thirty yards away. I was round first with my revolver, and the sergeant had a tommy-gun - were they surprised! I called on them to "jettez-vous à la planche" but they seemed to be a bit slow on the uptake. One of them lifted a rifle and I'm afraid he hadn't time to be sorry. This was a sort of HQ place, typewriters, ammunition, revolvers, bombs and, more to the point, beer and food. We had been going about six hours and we were ready for it. While we were dining the phone rang. We didn't answer but followed the wire and got another bull - four machine-guns, two light machine-guns, two mortars and fifty more prisoners. We lost only two men (sounds like a German communiqué). It was a long time since I had a day like it. Eventually, about eight hours later, we came back through the Aussie lines. We were rather tired so the prisoner laddies kindly carried the booty and equipment. The rest of the story can keep until I see you. I am getting rather tired of this country (Egypt). The job is not bad, but I can't stand the natives! [2]

As elements of the Commando had returned throughout the night, Geoffrey Keyes and X Party had held their position. Keyes reported the closing stages of the operation in his report:

> Next morning the 10th we saw through our glasses the French in Aiteniye surrender to Capt More, who had been captured the night before trying to reach us, on the approach of Australian troops and carriers from the direction of the road. Capt More's party about three officers and sixteen strong then joined me, and at 1200hrs I was ordered to withdraw leaving the Redoubt to the Australians.[3]

By 1200hrs on 10 June the Australian 21st Brigade had crossed the river in sufficient strength to advance through the position held by Geoffrey Keyes and the commandos of X Party. Ordered to withdraw, leaving the Redoubt to the Australians, Keyes instructed his men to collect what they could of their dead and wounded comrade's belongings as they crossed to the river and headed south. By 2300hrs the Commando was concentrated in the transit camp at Haifa.[4]

As Operation Exporter continued and the Allies advanced north towards Beirut, the Commando set sail for Cyprus at 1850hrs on 14 June, arriving in Famagusta at 0700hrs the following morning. Of the 456 men who had assembled on the same quay eleven days earlier, 130 had been killed or wounded in just over 29 hours of fighting. With nearly a third of the unit's operational strength being taken out of action it was a situation from which the Commando would never recover. Although their objectives changed as the situation evolved, and the despite the high number of casualties, the unit first taste of action had achieved some success. Despite the difficulties incurred during the landings; the lack of naval, air and limited artillery support; the shortage of detailed maps or photographs; a dramatic underestimate of the strength of the enemy; damaged wireless sets; and the perilous task of having to take on heavily fortified Troops by frontal assaults; the overall objective set by Pedder in his Operation Orders that the Unit would, "Seize and hold the enemy position long enough for the Australian Brigade to cross the river and pass through the position," had been achieved.

Major Geoffrey Keyes was pleased with the performance of his commandos, later writing in his report that the men, for their first time in action, behaved extremely well, and the Commanding Officer's training undoubtedly saved us much heavier casualties. Special mention should be made of the magnificent example set by Capt George Highland commanding No.3 Troop, "who remained cool and imperturbable under the barrage, and finally captured the redoubt"; and Lt Eric Garland "who by his complete disregard for all personal safety, steadied his men in the first barrage. He subsequently himself drew the fire of a sniper, who was causing severe casualties by exposing himself, located and shot him with a Bren gun. He was first to get across the river, and his determined efforts to cut the wire on the far side covered by grenades fired from a discharger-cap by one of his men, led to the surrender of the garrison. He also put the 75mm gun covering the river out of action by accurate fire from a 25mm A/T Gun, allowing the Australians to come up in support. His conduct throughout the action was worthy of the highest praise." [5] Keyes also singled out other men for whose individual achievements were worthy of special note and that mention should be made of Signaller A Reed, of No.3 Troop, "who while acting as number two to a Bren gun which became clogged with sand, took parts of the gun from the exposed position where it was mounted to better cover. He there cleaned them, returned to the gun under heavy fire, and reassembled the gun, getting into action himself as his corporal was killed beside him. He was one of the first boat load to cross the river and at all times behaved with great coolness." Keyes also had words of praise for L/Cpl Dilworth of 'C' Coy, 2/16 Bn, Australian Imperial Force, "who showed complete lack of regard for his own personal safety, and great dash and determination in carrying up with 3 of his section an assault boat, both under the preliminary barrage, and later under heavy machine gun fire. He brought his boat up to the forward troops, and later down to the river bank, one of his men being killed. While his men were paddling the first boat across, he ran back across the open under fire to bring up his Company Commander and the other boats. He returned again under fire to say that they would be some time coming up, and while his men went back for their equipment and arms, he came across with the 3rd boat, armed with a dead man's rifle. He then organised the crossing of later reinforcements, and the evacuation of the prisoners, on the river bank, which was still subjected to enemy shell and M.G. fire. His whole conduct was a very fine example to his section carrying the boat, and without his assistance, I would never have succeeded in getting a foothold north of the river. His two surviving men, whose names I never learnt, also deserve a share of the praise for their part in bringing up the boat, and ferrying my men across the river which was covered by fire. They both ran the first two trips each way."[6] Lt Bill Fraser, No. 8 Troop, who had been slightly concussed by a wound to the head during the raid, also had words of praise for some of his men including Sgts Nichol and Cheyne "who during the whole action behaved with extreme coolness under fire and repeatedly went alone into the woods to search for snipers. In addition, after I had been hit, they carried on with their sub-sections, and organised the withdrawal across the river, which was completed successfully."[7] Lt Eion McGonigal, No.4 Troop's Leader, singled out one of his attached men for special commendation, reporting that mention must be made of Gunner Percival, of No.1 Troop, "attached to us in the course of the action, during Monday afternoon he did excellent work bringing in the wounded and reconnoitring in a captured French truck, under heavy fire."[8] Capt Ian McDonald, in his report on the action of No.10 Troop commented that special mention should be made of L/Cpl Noble Sproule, "who covered our first withdrawal to the last possible moment with a captured machine gun and destroyed the gun before leaving it," an action that would get Sproule Mentioned in Dispatched; and Pte G Dove, "who did good work in bringing up spare ammunition under fire during the first attack in spite of being wounded."[9] Capt Ian Glennie, No.8 Troop Leader, commented in his report that L/Cpl Bob Tait, "whose extra coolness under fire, putting out of action one AFV and being instrumental in driving off six others, and lastly for his escape to Major Keyes' lines."[10] Capt George More, Z Party commander noted the exemplary devotion to duty of Lt G Parnacott, "who attempted to seize two ambulances whilst under heavy fire from enemy armoured cars," and L/Cpl Jackson RAMC, "who carried out his duties as medical orderly with very limited resources with courage and skill. Many wounded undoubtedly owe their lives to L/Cpl Jackson's exertions."[11]

For their courage, leadership and outstanding devotion to duty, Major Keyes, Capt More, and Lt Bryan were awarded the Military Cross, while Lt Garland received a second bar to his. Bryan's citation published in the London Gazette on 02 December 1941 read:

In the action at the Litani River in Syria on 9th June 1941, Lt Bryan was commanding a section of the force landed north of the river to disorganise enemy resistance from the rear. He led a party containing Sgt Worrall and five men against a French 75mm battery, under fire from concentrated machine gun offensive, captured the nearest gun with hand grenades. He directed its fire against the remaining guns, which were quickly silenced. The advance was continued, but Lt Bryan was very severely wounded through both legs, one being subsequently amputated. As a result he was taken prisoner but has since been liberated. His coolness and courage before and after being wounded was an inspiration to his men, and the capture of the battery greatly facilitated the crossing of the river, which it covered at very short range.[12]

Colonel Bob Laycock recommended George More for the Military Cross stating that "Capt More commanded his detachment with initiative, courage and skill. He was responsible for the capture of 60 prisoners, two Machine Guns and four 155mm Howitzers. Although his detachment became widely separated during the battle he was able to control them efficiently by personally visiting them often while under heavy fire and on one occasion had his motorcycle shot and destroyed under him."[13] Laycock also made recommendations for Lt Eric Garland to receive the Distinguished Service Order (DSO); however Garland was awarded a bar to the Military Cross that he had received for his actions at Dunkirk. Laycock wrote "Lt Garland displayed throughout the action cool and clear headed leadership and complete disregard for his own safety. He was the first individual to cross the river and personally led the party which cut the enemy wire on the far side under heavy fire. On one occasion by deliberately exposing himself he personally drew the fire of a sniper who was causing sever casualties, and on locating the enemy position, Lt Garland manned one of his Bren Guns and shot the sniper. Lt Garland also put out of action 75mm Gun, which was covering the river, by accurate fire from a captured anti tank gun."[14] For their many outstanding and courageous actions RSM Lewis Tevendale and LCpl Bob Tait were awarded the Distinguished Conduct Medal; and Sgt Frank Worrall the Military Medal. Worrall's citation in the London Gazette read:

In the action at the Litani River in Syria on June 9th 1941, this NCO was part of a force that landed north of the river to disorganize the enemy resistance from the rear. With Lt Bryan RE, his section Leader, he led a party of men against a French 75mm Battery, despite considerable opposition from concealed machine guns. Having captured the nearest gun with hand grenades, Sgt. Worall laid the gun with such accuracy that the remaining guns were rapidly silenced. When ordered to continue the advance, he put this gun out of action before moving on. Shortly afterwards he was severely wounded in the head, and taken prisoner, but has now been liberated. The dash and efficiency of this NCO in silencing the Battery had considerable effect on the successful crossing of the river, as the guns covered the approaches and crossings at very short range. Recommended for DCM or MM, awarded MM.[15]

CHAPTER 11
LITANI RIVER: REFLECTIONS AND COMMENTARY

Reg Harmer: "We had taken all our objectives, I would say by about 11 o'clock we had captured the whole lot, but we couldn't tell the Australians to advance...and we were cut off and we ran out of ammo, we only had so much that we could carry, and no grub and then we ran out of water and then we started using the French ammunition, rifles and guns. We really got a hiding in the afternoon, Richards, Parnacott, they were the two officers we lost, oh we lost some good boys there, Sgt O'Sullivan, Johnny King, we really got a bashing, cos we never really had nothing to fight them with."[1]

Sgt Charles Hill: "And so ended for us, a very tiring and hazardous adventure. From which we gained much experience. I might say that in the eyes of the Australians, if not the Press, we showed a fighting spirit which was admirable. The line was taken and held for at least thirty-one hours, when the agreed time was only eight hours. As a Military spokesman has said, "It was a complete Military success." But from the point of view of the actual participants it was 'too much of a good thing'. We held the enemy for twenty-three hours longer than food and ammunition was catered for and as a result lost a few hundred good men and a damned efficient Commanding Officer."[2]

Major Geoffrey Keyes: "One cannot visualise the Commando here without him (Dick Pedder). It is as though the mainspring had gone, which leaves a gap that will be impossible to fill.... The whole operation, though costly through no fault of ours, was a tremendous success, as admitted by all the powers that be and the credit for this most go entirely to Dick, for the way he trained us, and planned the operation. Before he was killed he had the satisfaction of knowing that his theories and training were right, although he never knew how successful we finally were. His party had succeeded in doing what was required first, and he was bringing them to help me, whom he knew was in trouble on his right, though he did not know where... The Army has lost a most farsighted officer, whose ability to learn from our failures and the successes of the enemy, made him one of the most successful trainers of men I have ever served under." [3]

Lt Col Harry Crawley Ross-Skinner: "Dick's (Pedder) death at the head of his Commando in the Battle of Litani River in Syria was a very sad loss to all of us. Those French, they let Hitler and his Germans go through them like a knife through butter; but when they resisted us, the Vichy French fought like tigers. In Syria in 1941, Petain was supposed to be going to allow Hitler to build air bases on the eastern seaboard of the Mediterranean. This had to be stopped. Dick and his Commandos did stop it, but Dick, sad to say, was one of those who did not come back. As usual it has to be THE BEST."[4]

Admiral Sir Walter Cowan: "I wish I could tell you more about your fight. G Keyes had lunch with me and told me a lot. Also saw Bob Laycock and he had to go and tell the King about it – anyhow it was by far the best achievement of any of the lot we journeyed out with and a success and ensured the success of the advance and it was so fitting that it fell to that battalion to carry it through as no one can contest the fact that they were by far the best trained, disciplined and soldier-like unit of the whole lot and the earnestness and selflessness and grit of all of you was a perpetual marvel and delight to me from when I first joined up with you." [5]

2/16 Australian Infantry Battalion, War Diary: "The crossing of the Litani River was the most difficult operation and the bulk of the credit goes to the SS Bn (Special Service Battalion) led by Major Keyes."[6]

Capt Longworth, Forward Observation Officer, 2/4th Australian Field Regiment: "On our way to the mouth of the river we passed what remained of portion of the gallant SS Battalion which had been met by a murderous hail of steel and H.E. (High Explosive) from French 75s, mortars and heavy machine guns. Their dead literally littered the beach."[7]

General Archibald Wavell: "After an extremely hard fight (the Australians) had crossed the Litani River on the coast. In this action a Commando from Cyprus effected a landing on the coast and assisted in the Australian success, although at the cost of somewhat heavy casualties."[8]

Winston Churchill: "Their advance (the Australians) was aided by a daring raid by No. 11 Commando, which was landed from the sea behind enemy lines. In this devoted stroke the Commando lost its leader, Colonel Pedder, who was killed with four of his officers, and there was nearly 100 casualties among the other ranks, over a quarter of its total strength."[9]

EPILOGUE

North Africa 1941

Within days of the Commando returning to Cyprus from Syria it became clear that it was likely to be disbanded, a fate that had already befallen both No. 7 and No.8 Commando.

Suitably trained replacements for those lost in Syria were difficult to come by and many original members of the Commando had returned to their old former units or volunteered for service in the newly-formed "L" Detachment, Special Air Service (SAS) and the Special Boat Section (SBS), who were very active in the region.

Geoffrey Keyes was promoted to acting Lieutenant-Colonel and took command of the Commando, which returned to Egypt after completion of garrison duties. However the Commando's disbandment was delayed as part of a daring attack on General Rommel's Headquarters in Cyrenica, 250 miles behind enemy lines. A force of six officers and 53 other ranks, led Keyes and Col Bob Laycock, embarked on H.M. Submarines Torbay and Talisman.

However during disembarkation at the landing site the submarines experienced difficulty in getting all the raiding force on to the beach, a combination of bad weather and misfortune resulted in only 36 getting ashore. With no choice but to change the plan it was decided that Laycock would stay at the landing site and that Keyes would lead No.1 detachment, which would attack Rommel's house and HQ at Beda Littoria; and that Lt Cook would take No.2 detachment and sabotage communications at the cross roads south of Cyrene. The detachments set off at 1900hrs on 15 November and after nearly two days of inhospitable terrain and weather they reached the objective.

At midnight on 17 November the attack was launched. Keyes, Capt Campbell and Sgt Jack Terry, walked up to the front door of the house and beat upon it, with Campbell demanding access in German. The door was opened by a sentry who was set upon and shot by Campbell, resulting in the occupants being alerted to the raiders, who had started to search the ground floor.

As they entered the second room the occupants were waiting for them and Geoffrey Keyes was met by a burst of fire which mortally wounded him. Terry emptied two magazines of his machine gun and Campbell threw a grenade before slamming the door shut. Between them they carried Geoffrey Keyes outside where he died almost immediately. In the process Campbell was hit by a stray bullet which broke his leg. Realising that he couldn't continue Campbell instructed Terry to round up the party and withdraw back to the beach, throwing grenades and causing as much damage as they could in the process.

They marched throughout the night and during the next day before reporting to Laycock at the original rendezvous.

Later in the evening, after being observed by an unfriendly Arab, Laycock ordered the party to move to the caves surrounding the beach where the re-embarkation on to the submarine Torbay was to take place.

Soon after dark Laycock spotted the submarine and started signalling immediately, but the sea was too rough and no re-embarkation would take place that night.

The next morning Laycock put the party in all-round defence, and with the weather clearing he was confident that re-embarkation would be possible that night.

However his optimism was short lived when enemy troops were observed approaching their position. With the enemy closing in and in superior numbers, Laycock ordered the party to split into groups and retreat into the Jebel-el-Akhdar hills. As Laycock made good his escape he paired up with Jack Terry and they would avoid capture for 41 days after landing on the beach, eventually rejoining British Forces at Cyrene on Christmas Day 1941. The remainder of the party weren't so lucky having either been killed or captured. Although three German officers and four other ranks were killed in the raid, the mission failed to capture Rommel, who as it turned out had not been at Beda Littoria at that time. For his actions Geoffrey Keyes was postumously awarded the Victoria Cross. For No.11 (Scottish) Commando the ill-fated raid was its final operation, and the Commando was disbanded.

Isle of Arran: 44 years later

In the days leading up to the weekend of 24/26 August 1985 the surviving members of No.11 (Scottish) Commando boarded the ferry and sailed across the Firth of Clyde from the Scottish mainland, just as they had done almost 45 years before in the summer of 1940. Although the years had slipped past, not much had changed on the island that the commandos proudly considered to be their "Base". Not the northern mountains and cliffs that had exhausted them; nor the speying rivers and coastal waters that had frozen them; nor the friendly island welcome that awaited them. Their first reunion since the war, around 50 former officers and men had made the journey to take part in the re-dedication of the Commando's plaque, with its Black Hackle centrepiece carved from a piece of bog oak from Machrie Moor, and with the units motto "No Quarter" engraved proudly below it. But that was not the only reason they had travelled from far and wide. They went for the conversations, the company and the comradeship, to remember the landladies who had mothered them and to thank the good people of Arran for their warmth and generosity. But most of all they went, as they would for the following 25 years, to remember with pride the comrades who they had trained, fought and died with, as officers and men of No.11 (Scottish) Commando.

Veterans at Brodick Castle, Isle of Arran, during a reunion

Photo courtesy of
Wilkinson Collection

Veterans during a reunion at the Arran Heritage Museum

Photo courtesy of
Wilkinson Collection

NOTES

Chapter 1

(1) Ministry of Defence Records Office – Humphries Collection
(2) Anonymous letter - Humphries Collection
(3) Humphries Collection - Extract from Harry's Book, Harry Ross-Skinner
(4) Churchill, W (2005 edn). *Their finest hour: the Second World War Vol.11,* London, Penguin
(5) Miller, R. (2004). *World War Two Commandos,* Life Time
(6) Messenger, C. (1985). *The Commandos 1940-1946,* London, William Kimber
(7) Churchill, W (2005 edn). *Their finest hour: the Second World War Vol.11,* London, Penguin
(8) Keyes, E. (1956). *Geoffrey Keyes,* London, George Newnes
(9) Interview Sir Thomas Macpherson, Dr Hamish Ross
(10) Saunders, H. S. (1949). The Green Beret - The Story of the Commandos, 1940-1945. London,
(11) Lappin, A.G. (1996). *Black Hackle: The Story of the 11th (Scottish) Commando,* Unpublished
(12) Keyes, E. (1956). *Geoffrey Keyes,* London, George Newnes
(13) Interview Reg Harmer
(14) Interview Reg Harmer
(15) Keyes, E. (1956). *Geoffrey Keyes,* London, George Newnes
(16) Lappin, A.G. (1996). *Black Hackle: The Story of the 11th (Scottish) Commando,* Unpublished
(17) Interview Sir Thomas Macpherson

Chapter 2

(1) Keyes, E. (1956). *Geoffrey Keyes*, London, George Newnes
(2) Ross, H. (2003). *Paddy Mayne,* Stroud, Sutton
(3) Interview Sir Thomas Macpherson, Dr Hamish Ross
(4) Lappin, A.G. (1996). *Black Hackle: The Story of the 11th (Scottish) Commando,* Unpublished
(5) Interview Reg Harmer
(6) Conversation with Jessie Turner
(7) Humphries Collection
(8) Keyes, E. (1956). *Geoffrey Keyes,* London, George Newnes
(9) Interview Sir Thomas Macpherson, Dr Hamish Ross
(10) Interview Sir Thomas Macpherson
(11) Interview Reg Harmer
(12) Ross, H. (2003). *Paddy Mayne,* Stroud, Sutton
(13) Interview Reg Harmer
(14) Interview Reg Harmer
(15) Keyes, E. (1956). *Geoffrey Keyes,* London, George Newnes
(16) Lappin, A.G. (1996). *Black Hackle: The Story of the 11th (Scottish) Commando,* Unpublished
(17) Gerald Bryan Collection
(18) Keyes, E. (1956). *Geoffrey Keyes,* London, George Newnes
(19) Keyes, E. (1956). *Geoffrey Keyes,* London, George Newnes
(20) Interview Reg Harmer
(21) Keyes, E. (1956). *Geoffrey Keyes,* London, George Newnes
(22) Interview Sir Thomas Macpherson
(23) Humphries Collection
(24) Interview Reg Harmer
(25) Moreman, T. (2006). *British Commandos 1940-1946,* Osprey
(26) Keyes, E. (1956). *Geoffrey Keyes,* London, George Newnes
(27) Keyes, E. (1956). *Geoffrey Keyes,* London, George Newnes

Chapter 3

(1) Interview Sir Thomas Macpherson, Dr Hamish Ross
(2) George More Diary, 1941
(3) Interview Sir Thomas Macpherson, Dr Hamish Ross
(4) Interview Reg Harmer
(5) George More Diary, 1941
(6) George More Diary, 1941
(7) Interview Sir Thomas Macpherson
(8) Interview Sir Thomas Macpherson
(9) Arran Heritage Museum, No.11 (Scottish) Commando Collection
(10) George More Diary, 1941
(11) George More Diary, 1941
(12) No 11 (Scottish) Commando War Diary, 1941. PRO WO 218/171
(13) Wynter, H.W. (2001). *Special Forces In The Desert War 1940-43,* Kew, Public Record Office
(14) No 11 (Scottish) Commando War Diary, 1941. PRO WO 218/171
(15) George More Diary, 1941
(16) Wynter, H.W. (2001). *Special Forces In The Desert War 1940-43,* Kew, Public Record Office

Chapter 4

(1) No 11 (Scottish) Commando War Diary, PRO WO 218/171
(2) Interview Sir Thomas Macpherson
(3) Gerald Bryan Collection
(4) Correspondence received from Jim Bogle
(5) Interview Sir Thomas Macpherson, Dr Hamish Ross
(6) Stilwell, A. (ed.) (2004). *The Second World War in Flames*, Osprey
(7) Neillands, R. (1990). *The Raiders: Army Commandos 1940-46* London, Fontana
(8) Wynter, H.W. (2001). *Special Forces In The Desert War 1940-43*, Kew, Public Record Office
(9) Correspondence received from Jim Bogle
(10) Gerald Bryan Collection
(11) Neillands, R. (1990). *The Raiders: Army Commandos 1940-46* London, Fontana
(12) Australian War Memorial, 21 Infantry Brigade War Diary, 52-8-2-21

Chapter 5

(1) George More Diary, 1941
(2) Wynter, H.W. (2001) *Special Forces In The Desert War 1940-43,* Kew, Public Record Office
(3) Stilwell, A. (ed.) (2004). *The Second World War in Flames,* Osprey
(4) Keegan, J. (ed.) (2005). *Churchill's Generals,* London, Cassell
(5) Ross, H. (2003). *Paddy Mayne,* Stroud, Sutton
(6) Australia in the War of 1939-1945, Volume II, Chapter 16
(7) Australia in the War of 1939-1945, Volume II, Chapter 16
(8) Australia in the War of 1939-1945, Volume II, Chapter 16
(9) Australian War Memorial, 21 Infantry Brigade War Diary, 52-8-2-21
(10) Australia in the War of 1939-1945, Volume II, Chapter 16
(11) Wynter, H.W. (2001). *Special Forces In The Desert War 1940-43,* Kew, Public Record Office
(12) Wynter, H.W. (2001). *Special Forces In The Desert War 1940-43,* Kew, Public Record Office

Chapter 6

(1) Wynter, H.W. (2001). *Special Forces In The Desert War 1940-43*, Kew, Public Record Office
(2) No 11 (Scottish) Commando War Diary, PRO WO 218/171
(3) Australia in the War of 1939-1945, Volume II, Chapter 16
(4) Australia in the War of 1939-1945, Volume II, Chapter 16
(5) Australian War Memorial, 21 Infantry Brigade War Diary, 52-8-2-21
(6) Australian War Memorial, 21 Infantry Brigade War Diary, 52-8-2-21
(7) Australia in the War of 1939-1945, Volume II, Chapter 18
(8) Australian War Memorial, 2/16 Infantry Battalion War Diary, 52-8-3-16

Chapter 7

(1) Major Keyes, G. X Party Report, 1941. PRO WO 218/171
(2) Lt. Collar, M.H. Beach Landing Report, 1941. PRO WO 218/171
(3) Major Keyes, G. X Party Report, 1941. PRO WO 218/171
(4) Keyes, E. (1956). *Geoffrey Keyes*, London, George Newnes
(5) Australian War Memorial, 2/16 Infantry Battalion War Diary, 52-8-3-16
(6) Keyes, E. (1956). *Geoffrey Keyes*, London, George Newnes
(7) Australian War Memorial, 2/16 Infantry Battalion War Diary, 52-8-3-16
(8) Major Keyes, G. X Party Report, 1941. PRO WO 218/171
(9) Major Keyes, G. X Party Report, 1941. PRO WO 218/171
(10) Australian War Memorial, 2/16 Infantry Battalion War Diary, 52-8-3-16
(11) Wynter, H.W. (2001). *Special Forces In The Desert War 1940-43*, Kew, Public Record Office
(12) Keyes, E. (1956). *Geoffrey Keyes*, London, George Newnes
(13) Keyes, E. (1956). *Geoffrey Keyes*, London, George Newnes

Chapter 8

(1) Gerald Bryan Collection
(2) Neillands, R. (1990). *The Raiders: Army Commandos 1940-46* London, Fontana
(3) RSM Tevendale, L. Y Party Report, 1941. PRO WO 218/171
(4) Gerald Bryan Collection
(5) RSM Tevendale, L. Y Party Report, 1941. PRO WO 218/171
(6) Neillands, R. (1990). *The Raiders: Army Commandos 1940-46* London, Fontana
(7) Capt Glennie, I. Troop Report (1941). PRO WO 218/171
(8) Ross, H. (2003). *Paddy Mayne,* Stroud, Sutton
(9) Ross, H. (2003) *Paddy Mayne,* Stroud, Sutton
(10) Ross, H. (2003) *Paddy Mayne,* Stroud, Sutton
(11) Wynter, H.W. (2001). *Special Forces In The Desert War 1940-43,* Kew, Public Record Office
(12) Wynter, H.W. (2001). *Special Forces In The Desert War 1940-43,* Kew, Public Record Office
(13) Lt Fraser, W. Troop Report, 1941. PRO WO 218/171
(14) Wynter, H.W. (2001). *Special Forces In The Desert War 1940-43,* Kew, Public Record Office
(15) Wynter, H.W. (2001). *Special Forces In The Desert War 1940-43,* Kew, Public Record Office
(16) Ross, H. (2003). *Paddy Mayne,* Stroud, Sutton
(17) Ross, H. (2003). *Paddy Mayne,* Stroud, Sutton
(18) Australian War Memorial, 21 Infantry Brigade War Diary, 52-8-2-21
(19) Ross, H. (2003). *Paddy Mayne,* Stroud, Sutton
(20) Neillands, R. (1990). *The Raiders: Army Commandos 1940-46* London, Fontana
(21) RSM Tevendale, L. Y Party Report, 1941. PRO WO 218/171
(22) RSM Tevendale, L. Y Party Report, 1941. PRO WO 218/171
(23) Gerald Bryan Collection
(24) Gerald Bryan Collection
(25) Neillands, R. (1990). *The Raiders: Army Commandos 1940-46* London, Fontana
(26) Gerald Bryan Collection

(27) RSM Tevendale, L. Y Party Report, 1941. PRO WO 218/171
(28) Gerald Bryan Collection
(29) Gerald Bryan Collection

Chapter 9

(1) Sir Thomas Macpherson Collection – Notes from the left flank
(2) Capt. More, G. Z Party Report, 1941. PRO WO218/171
(3) Capt. More, G. Z Party Report, 1941. PRO WO218/171
(4) George More Diary, 1941
(5) Capt. McDonald, I. 10 Troop Report, 1941. PRO WO218/171
(6) Capt. McDonald, I. 10 Troop Report, 1941. PRO WO218/171
(7) Sir Thomas Macpherson Collection – Notes from the left flank
(8) Keyes, E. (1956). *Geoffrey Keyes,* London, George Newnes
(9) Lappin, A.G. (1996). *Black Hackle: The Story of the 11th (Scottish) Commando,* Unpublished
(10) Asher, M. (2004). *Get Rommel,* London, Cassell
(11) Interview Reg Harmer
(12) Capt. More, G. Z Party Report, 1941. PRO WO218/171
(13) Capt. More, G. Z Party Report, 1941. PRO WO218/171
(14) Charles Hill Collection
(15) Charles Hill Collection
(16) Charles Hill Collection
(17) Lt. McGonigal, E. 4 Troop Report, 1941. PRO WO218/171
(18) Lt. McGonigal, E. 4 Troop Report, 1941. PRO WO218/171
(19) Capt. More, G. Z Party Report, 1941. PRO WO218/171
(20) Charles Hill Collection
(21) Capt Glennie, I. A Section, 8 Troop Report, 1941. PRO WO218/171
(22) Capt. More, G. Z Party Report, 1941. PRO WO218/171
(23) Capt. McDonald, I. 10 Troop Report, 1941. PRO WO218/171
(24) Capt. McDonald, I. 10 Troop Report, 1941. PRO WO218/171

(25) Sir Thomas Macpherson Collection – Notes from the left flank
(26) Sir Thomas Macpherson Collection
(27) Sir Thomas Macpherson Collection – Notes from the left flank
(28) Wynter, H.W. (2001). *Special Forces In The Desert War 1940-43*, Kew, Public Record Office
(29) Lt. McGonigal, E. 4 Troop Report, 1941. PRO WO218/171
(30) Charles Hill Collection
(31) Capt. McDonald, I. 10 Troop Report, 1941. PRO WO218/171
(32) Wright, C. (2002). French and Commonwealth OOB's for Operation Exporter
(33) Sir Thomas Macpherson Collection – Notes from the left flank
(34) Australian War Memorial, 2/16 Infantry Battalion War Diary, 52-8-3-16
(35) Capt. McDonald, I. 10 Troop Report, 1941. PRO WO218/171
(36) Capt. McDonald, I. 10 Troop Report, 1941. PRO WO218/171
(37) Lt. Fraser, W. B Section, 8 Troop Report, 1941. PRO WO218/171
(38) Lt. Fraser, W. B Section, 8 Troop Report, 1941. PRO WO218/171
(39) Capt. More, G. Z Party Report, 1941. PRO WO218/171
(40) Charles Hill Collection
(41) Capt Glennie, I. A Section, 8 Troop Report, 1941. PRO WO218/171
(42) Capt Glennie, I. A Section, 8 Troop Report, 1941. PRO WO218/171
(43) Capt. More, G. Z Party Report, 1941. PRO WO218/171
(44) Capt Glennie, I. A Section, 8 Troop Report, 1941. PRO WO218/171
(45) Capt Glennie, I. A Section, 8 Troop Report, 1941. PRO WO218/171
(46) Capt. McDonald, I. 10 Troop Report, 1941. PRO WO218/171

(47) Sir Thomas Macpherson Collection
(48) Lt. McGonigal, E. 4 Troop Report, 1941. PRO WO218/171
(49) Lt. McGonigal, E. 4 Troop Report, 1941. PRO WO218/171
(50) Lt. McGonigal, E. 4 Troop Report, 1941. PRO WO218/171
(51) Capt Glennie, I. A Section, 8 Troop Report, 1941. PRO WO218/171
(52) Capt Glennie, I. A Section, 8 Troop Report, 1941. PRO WO218/171
(53) Capt Glennie, I. A Section, 8 Troop Report, 1941. PRO WO218/171
(54) Capt Glennie, I. A Section, 8 Troop Report, 1941. PRO WO218/171
(55) Capt. More, G. Z Party Report, 1941. PRO WO218/171
(56) Capt Glennie, I. A Section, 8 Troop Report, 1941. PRO WO218/171
(57) Capt. More, G. Z Party Report, 1941. PRO WO218/171
(58) Charles Hill Collection
(59) Capt Glennie, I. A Section, 8 Troop Report, 1941. PRO WO218/171
(60) Sir Thomas Macpherson Collection – 10 Troop withdrawal
(61) Sir Thomas Macpherson Collection – Notes from the left flank
(62) Sir Thomas Macpherson Collection – Notes from the left flank
(63) Letter form Tom Herd
(64) Sir Thomas Macpherson Collection

Chapter 10

(1) RSM Tevendale, L. Y Party Report, 1941. PRO WO 218/171
(2) Bradford, R. and Dillon, M. (1987). *Rogue Warrior of the SAS*, London, John Murray
(3) Major Keyes, G. (1941). X Party Report. PRO WO 218/171
(4) Wynter, H.W. (2001). *Special Forces In The Desert War 1940-43*, Kew, Public Record Office
(5) Major Keyes, G. X Party Report, 1941. PRO WO 218/171
(6) Major Keyes, G. X Party Report, 1941. PRO WO 218/171
(7) Lt. Fraser, W. B Section, 8 Troop Report, 1941. PRO WO218/171
(8) Lt. McGonigal, E. 4 Troop Report, 1941. PRO WO218/171
(9) Capt. McDonald, I. 10 Troop Report, 1941. PRO WO218/171
(10) Capt. Glennie, I. A Section, 8 Troop Report, 1941. PRO WO218/171
(11) Capt. More, G. Z Party Report, 1941. PRO WO218/171
(12) London Gazette, 02.12.41
(13) WO/373/27/525.
(14) WO/373/27/521
(15) London Gazette, 02.12.41

Chapter 11

(1) Interview Reg Harmer
(2) Charles Hill Collection
(3) Keyes, E. (1956). *Geoffrey Keyes,* London, George Newnes
(4) Humphries Collection - Extract from Harry's Book, Harry Ross-Skinner
(5) Gerald Bryan Collection
(6) Australian War Memorial, 2/16 Infantry Battalion War Diary, 52-8-3-16
(7) Australia in the War of 1939-1945, Volume II
(8) Gerald Bryan Collection
(9) Churchill, W. (2005edn). *The Grand Alliance: The Second World War Volume 111,* London, Penguin

BIBLIOGRAPHY

Allan, S. (2007). *Commando Country,* National War Museums
Asher, M. (2004). *Get Rommel,* London Cassell
Almonds Windmill, L. (2001). *Gentleman Jim: The Wartime Story of a Founder of the SAS,* London, Constable
Bradford, R. and Dillon, M. (1987). *Rogue Warrior of the SAS,* London, John Murray
Brown, G. A. (1991). *Commando Gallantry Awards of WW,* London, Anthony Rowe Ltd
Byrne, J.V. (1986). *The General Salutes a Soldier,* London, Robert Hale
Churchill, W. (2005edn). *The Grand Alliance: The Second World War Volume 111,* London, Penguin
Churchill, W (2005 edn). *Their finest hour: the Second World War Vol.11,* London, Penguin
Cooksey, J. (2005). *Operation Chariot: The Raid on St. Nazaire,* Pen and Sword
Duggan, S. (2001). *Commando: The elite fighting forces of the Second World War,* Macmillan
Durnford-Slater, J. (1953). *Command: Memoirs of a Fighting Commando in World War Two,* London, Greenhill
Hampshire, C.A. (1983). *The Beachhead Commando,* London, William Kimber
Harclerode, P. and Reynolds, D. (2003). *Commando,* Stroud, Sutton
Jordan, D. and West, A. (2004). *Atlas of World War Two,* Silverdale Books
Gilchrist, D. (1960). *Castle Commando,* Lochaber District Council
Keegan, J. (ed.) (2005). *Churchill's Generals,* London, Cassell
Keyes, E. (1956). *Geoffrey Keyes,* London, George Newnes
Laffin, J. (1999). *Raiders: Great Exploits of the Second World War,* Stroud, Sutton Publishing
Lappin, A.G. (1996). *Black Hackle: The Story of the 11th (Scottish) Commando,* Unpublished
Ladd, J. (1978). *Commandos & Rangers of WW2,* London, Book Club Associates
Lucas, J. (1982). *War in the desert,* Arms and Armour Press

MacDonald, C. (1993). *The Lost Battle: Crete 1941*, London, Macmillan
Messenger, C. (1985). *The Commandos 1940-1946*, London, William Kimber
Messenger, C. (1988). *The Middle East Commandos*, London, William Kimber
Miller, R. (2004). *World War Two Commandos*, Life Time
Moreman, T. (2006). *British Commandos 1940-1946*, Osprey
Mortimer, G. (2004). *Stirling's Men*, London, Cassell
Neillands, R. (1990). *The Raiders: Army Commandos 1940-46* London, Fontana
Oatts. L.B. (1963). *Proud Heritage: The Story of the Highland Light Infantry, Glasgow,* The House of Grant
Porch, D. (2005). *Hitler's Mediterranean Gamble*, London, Cassell
Saunders, H. St. G. (1949). *The Green Beret - The Story of the Commandos, 1940-1945* London, Michael Joesph
Stilwell, A. (ed.) (2004). *The Second World War in Flames*, Osprey
Wynter, H.W. (2001). *Special Forces In The Desert War 1940-43*, Kew, Public Record Office

Official Collections

PRO WO218/171: No.11 (Scottish) Commando War Diary
AWM 52-8-2-21: 21 Australian Infantry Brigade War Diary
AWM 52-8-3-16: 2/16 Australian Infantry Battalion War Diary

Personal Collections, Diaries and Memoirs

Charles Hill Collection – courtesy of Mrs Agnes Hill
George More 1941 Diary – courtesy of Henry More
Gerald Bryan Collection - courtesy of Gerald Bryan
Humphries Collection – courtesy of Mrs Elizabeth Humphries
Norman Wilkinson Collection – courtesy of Ian Ormerod-Wilkinson
Sir Thomas Macpherson Collection – courtesy of Sir Tommy Macpherson

Interviews, Letters and Correspondence

Eric Garland
Gerald Bryan
James Swanson – courtesy of Mr A.J. Swanson
Jim Bogle
Jimmy Lawson
Jimmy Storie
Jock Herd – courtesy of Tom Herd
Joe Gorman
Reg Harmer
Sir Tommy Macpherson

Litani River

For more information please visit:
www.litaniriver.com

Litani River

www.ingramcontent.com/pod-product-compliance
Lightning Source LLC
Chambersburg PA
CBHW032118090426
42743CB00007B/386